LONGMAN

English Works

WORKBOOK

1

Sally Burgess

Robert O'Neill

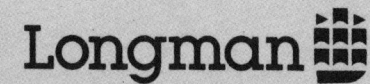

Addison Wesley Longman Limited
Edinburgh Gate
Harlow
Essex CM20 2JE
England
and Associated Companies throughout the world.

First published 1993
Fourth impression 1996

Set in 10 on 11pt Garamond ITC

Produced through Longman Malaysia, BVS

ISBN 0 582 08542 X

Designed by Ken Vail Graphic Design

Illustrated by Julie Douglas, John Erwood,
Sue Faulkes (Eikon Ltd), Duncan Smith and Gary Wing.

Acknowledgements

Dictionary definitions (pages 36, 42 and 49) are taken
from the *Longman Active Study Dictionary*.

We are grateful to the following for permission to
reproduce copyright photographs:

Greg Evans Photolibrary for page 26; Longman
Photographic Unit for page 40; Tony Stone Worldwide
for page 5 (bottom); Telegraph Colour Library for page
5 (top).

Contents

Times and places

1

Match the questions (1–6) with the answers (a–f).

1 What languages do they speak in Switzerland? __d__

2 Is Kuala Lumpur a city or a country? _____

3 What country do they come from? _____

4 Where is São Paolo? _____

5 What languages does she speak? _____

6 It's four o'clock here in London. What time is it in Paris? _____

a) It's in Brazil.
b) Five o'clock.
c) Germany.
d) French, German and Italian.
e) It's a city in Malaysia.
f) German and Spanish.

Personal information

2

Choose the correct word.

1 Tessa Saunders __is__ British.
   a) is   b) am   c) are

2 _____ is 29.
   a) She   b) He   c) They

3 Tessa lives _____ London.
   a) in   b) at   c) on

4 _____ address is 12 Greenwood Street, Wimbledon, London.
   a) His   b) Her   c) Their

5 Roger Mitchum is _____ London.
   a) of   b) on   c) from

6 _____ lives in San Francisco now.
   a) She   b) He   c) They

7 _____ address is 474 Gonzalez Avenue, San Francisco, California.
   a) Her   b) His   c) Their

8 What about you? What's _____ address?
   a) my   b) your   c) their

Questions and answers

3

Look at what the man says (1–6). Find Tessa's answers (a–f).

1 Good evening, Madam. Can I help you? __c__

2 And what is your first name, please? _____

3 Oh, yes. Here it is. Ms T Saunders. How long are you staying, Ms Saunders? _____

4 Please write your name and your passport number on this form. _____

5 Yes, that's right. Your room number is three fourteen. _____

6 Three fourteen. Here's your key. _____

a) For three nights.
b) Pardon?
c) Yes. My name is Saunders. I have a reservation.
d) Thank you.
e) Tessa.
f) Where? Here?

Numbers

4

Write these hotel room numbers in words.

1   236   two thirty-six

2   159   _____

3   704   _____

4   1203   _____

5   1477   _____

6   409   _____

Questions and answers

5

Make questions.

1   she doing what is   _What is she doing?_

2   wearing she is what _____

3   she who is _____

4   does she live where _____

5   is how she old _____

Now look at the picture in exercise 3 and at exercise 2 again and answer the questions above.

1   _She's taking her key._

2 _____

3 _____

4 _____

5 _____

Grammar: prepositions

6

Look at the picture in exercise 3 again and choose the correct word.

Tessa is (1) *in*/*on* a hotel. She is standing (2) *at*/*on* the reception desk. She is taking her key (3) *to*/*from* the receptionist. He is writing her passport number (4) *to*/*in* the hotel register. There are some pens and pencils (5) *in*/*on* a box and a clock (6) *in*/*on* the wall. There is a porter (7) *near*/*at* the lift.

Personal information

7

Read about Tom MacDonald and Kate Crawford. Then answer the questions below with 'Yes', 'No' or 'I don't know'.

Hello. My name is Tom MacDonald. I'm an engineer. I work for a Japanese company in England. I come from Canada but I live in London. I'm twenty-nine years old and I'm single.

My name is Kate Crawford. I'm twenty-seven and I'm Australian. I work for an international bank in London. I like my job very much.

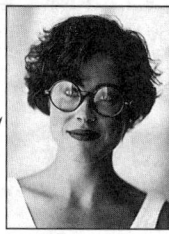

1   Is he an engineer? _Yes_

2   Is he married? _____

3   Is she married? _____

4   Is she from Canada? _____

5   Is he from Canada? _____

6   Does she work in a bank? _____

7   Does she like her job? _____

8   Does he like his job? _____

9   Do they speak English? _____

Review

8

Complete the sentences with *His* or *Her*, *He* or *She*.

1 __His__ first name is Tom.
2 ____ first name is Kate.
3 ____ works for a bank.
4 ____ is an engineer.
5 ____ surname is MacDonald.
6 ____ surname is Crawford.
7 ____ works for a Japanese company.
8 ____ comes from Canada.
9 ____ likes her job very much.

9

What about you? Complete these sentences about yourself.

1 My name is _____ .
2 I am _____ years old.
3 I come from _____ .
4 I live in _____ .
5 I work for _____ .
6 I (like/don't like) _____ my job very much.
7 I am (single/married) _____ .

10

Fill in this form with information about yourself.

⌒ *Hotel Albion* ⌒

Surname ....:..
Other names ....
Age .... *Nationality* ....
Marital status: single/married

Present address:...................................
city/town ....
....
country ....

Please sign below
....

11

Make questions.

1 you married are __Are you married?__
2 tennis play can you _____
3 you where from are _____
4 old you how are _____
5 do you what do _____

Vocabulary: people and work

12

Match the words for jobs (1–8) with the definitions (a–h):

1 mechanic /mɪˈkænɪk/ *n* __f__
2 hotel receptionist /həʊˈtel rɪsepʃənˌst/ *n* ____
3 teacher /ˈtiːtʃəʳ/ *n* ____
4 bank clerk /bæŋk klɑːk/ *n* ____
5 porter /ˈpɔːtəʳ/ *n* ____
6 sales assistant /seɪlz əsɪstənt/ *n* ____
7 secretary /ˈsekrəˌtəri/ *n* ____
8 waiter /ˈweɪtəʳ/ *n* ____

a) prepares letters, keeps records and arranges meetings for the boss
b) teaches children or adults at school or university
c) carries travellers' bags at railway stations, airports or hotels
d) serves customers in a shop or department store
e) serves customers in a bank
f) repairs machines, especially cars
g) serves food at the tables in a restaurant
h) recieves people arriving in a hotel

Word families

13

Find the word that doesn't belong.

1 (Germany) Italian Japanese Greek
2 desk chair clock jacket
3 near from one at
4 office house factory shop
5 water waiter engineer nurse

14 Just for fun: crossword

Across

1 She's from China. She speaks _____ .(7)
6 He's from Spain. __ she from Spain too? (2)
8 Paris is a big city in _____.(6)
9 A: Can you drive a ___? (3)
10 B: ___, I can't. (2)
11 'What's _____ first name, Mr Mitchum?' (4)
12 July, August, September, _____ (7)
14 Does Tessa _____ in an office? (4)
16 The opposite of *stand*. (3)
17 'Tea __ coffee?' (2)
18 Tom MacDonald lives _____ his office. (4)
22 _____ you work in a factory? (2)
23 A place where you can eat. (10)
27 Tessa is standing __ the reception desk. (2)
28 A: How do you _____Wimbledon?
   B: W–I–M–B–L–E–D–O–N (5)
30 In the picture of the hotel there are some pencils on the _____ . (4)
31 A: Here's your key, Mr Mitchum. B: _____ you. (5)
33 Do you use a wordprocessor __ a typewriter? (2)
34 A: Is there __ airport in your city? (2)
36 B: ___, there is. (3)
38 'I have a reservation for a single _____.' (4)
39 '__ name is Mitchum.' (2)
40 I, me, my; ___, us, our. (2)
41 Opposite of *difficult*. (4)
42 Doctors and _____ work in hospitals. (6)

Down

1 Tokyo isn't a country. It's a _____. (4)
2 Is there a bank _____ here? (4)
3 We wear shoes and _____ on our feet. (5)
4 🗅 (4)
5 A: Can I see your passport, please?
   B: _____ you are. (4)
7 'A single room with a _____.' (6)
8 Tessa is _____ Britain. (4)
13 I can't play golf, ___ I can play tennis. (3)
14 Monday, Tuesday, _____. (9)
15 Do you _____ the French word for *goodbye*? (4)
19 You go there when you arrive at a hotel or a company.(9)
20 The language they speak in Italy.(7)
21 Opposite of *question*.(6)
24 New York is a big city in the ___.(3)
25 'Can I ___ you some questions?' (3)
26 The number after *nine*.(3)
29 'My daughter _____ French at school.'(6)
30 The man is knocking at the _____.(4)
32 'Your room number is seven oh two. Here's your ___. (3)
35 Opposite of *old*.(3)
37 'What can you ___ in the picture?'(3)

1

Conversation management

1

Choose the best answer.

1 Good morning.
a) No.
b) Yes.
c) Good morning.

2 Hello. My name is Kate Crawford. I work for Anglo-International Bank.
a) Hi.
b) How do you do?
c) You are well.

3 Excuse me. Are you Tom MacDonald?
a) Yes, that's right.
b) I am Tom.
c) Yes, it is.

4 How do you do?
a) Yes, I do.
b) How do you do?
c) I work in a bank.

5 How are you this morning?
a) I'm fine, thanks. How are you?
b) How do you do?
c) Yes, I am.

6 Would you like a cup of coffee?
a) No, I don't.
b) No, I don't like.
c) No, thanks.

2

Make questions.

1 You are a student.
   <u>Are you a student?</u>

2 English is easy.
   _____

3 You are from where.
   _____

4 You can speak English.
   _____

5 I can help you.
   _____

6 You are staying where.
   _____

Vocabulary: opposites

3

Correct the mistakes in these sentences.

1 London is a ~~small~~ city. ___big___

2 I don't know London at all. This is my last visit here. _____

3 I can't carry this bag. It is very light. _____

4 I like this hotel very much. It is very bad. _____

4

Correct the mistakes in these sentences, too.

1 This is Tom MacDonald. ~~She~~ works for a Japanese company in England. ___He___

2 Look at this woman. Their name is Françoise. ____

3 He is French. _____

4 Françoise and Tom are at the airport in Lille. Lille is a city. He is in France. _____

5 Françoise is talking to Tom. She is asking them a question. _____

Meeting people

5

Read the conversation between Françoise and Tom. What are the missing words or phrases?

Françoise: Excuse me. (1) __Are you__ Tom MacDonald?

Tom: Yes, that's right.

Françoise: Hello. My name's Françoise Burnel. I'm from Poirel International.

Tom: Pleased to meet you.

Françoise: A car is coming for us in a few minutes. (2) _____ I get you a coffee or a cold drink?

Tom: No, thanks. I'm fine for the moment.

(3) _____ I staying? I mean, which hotel?

Françoise: The Hotel Flaubert. (4) _____ know it?

Tom: No, I don't. This is my (5) _____ to Lille.

Françoise: (6) _____ are you staying?

Tom: For two nights.

Grammar: How much/How many

6

Choose the correct alternative.

1 (How much)/How many coffee do you want?

2 How much/How many people work for your company?

3 How much/How many nights are you staying?

4 How much/How many money do you want to change?

5 How much/How many is a single room with a shower?

6 How much/How many English do you know?

7 How much/How many languages do you speak?

Grammar: pronouns and possessive adjectives

7

Complete the sentences.

1 Look. There's Tom MacDonald. Do you know __him__ ?

2 I'm writing a letter to Tessa Saunders. What's _____ address?

3 That's Kate Crawford over there. Do you know _____ ?

4 We live near your hotel. Can you come to _____ house for dinner this Saturday?

5 They are staying at the Hotel Excelsior. We are meeting _____ there.

6 I like the grey trousers. How much do _____ cost?

7 Those shoes are very nice. Have you got _____ in size thirty-eight?

8 We are arriving in the afternoon. Can you meet _____ at the airport?

9 This is my first visit to San Francisco. Is _____ an interesting city?

10 Can you help _____? My bag is very heavy.

Vocabulary: clothes

8

Choose the correct word.

1 A: What number/(size)/letter do you take?
   B: A thirty-eight skirt and a forty jacket.

2 A: What/Why/When colour?
   B: Dark red or light brown.

3 A: What/How/Where much do you want to spend?
   B: About two hundred pounds.

9

Look at the picture and write in the word next to each item of clothing.

1 skirt
2 _____
3 _____
4 _____
5 _____
6 _____
7 _____
8 _____
9 _____
10 _____
11 _____

10

Put the ticks in the correct columns.

	Men	Women
suit	✓	✓
dress		
trousers		
tie		
shirt		
skirt		
coat		
blouse		
jacket		
tights		

11

Find the word that doesn't belong.

1 sandals (gloves) shoes boots
2 blouse t-shirt shirt jeans
3 underpants vest raincoat bra
4 cotton hat wool silk
5 jacket sleeve collar pocket

12

Complete the dialogue.

A: Can I help (1) __you__, madam?

B: Yes, I'm (2) _____ for a blouse.

   (3) _____ you got this one

   in my (4) _____?

A: What size do you take?

B: I'm a size forty, I think.

A: I'm afraid we don't have your (5) _____ in

   this colour. Perhaps the pink or the green?

B: Can you show (6) _____ the pink blouse?

A: Here you are, madam.

B: It's very pretty. How (7) _____ is it?

A: Forty-five pounds.

B: Mmm. Can I try (8) _____ on?

2

Conversation management

1

Match the questions (1–8) with the answers (a–h).

1 Can I ask you a few questions? __g__

2 When do you usually get up in the morning? ____

3 How do you get to work? ____

4 How long does it take you to get there? ____

5 When do you leave work? ____

6 What do you do in the evening? ____

7 When do you usually go to bed? ____

8 How much sleep do you usually get? ____

a) Never before five.

b) At about eleven pm on weekdays and a little later at the weekend.

c) Usually about seven but on Sundays at eight or nine.

d) About eight hours.

e) It depends on the traffic. Usually forty-five minutes.

f) Sometimes I read or watch television. On Saturdays I meet friends or go to the cinema.

g) Of course. Go ahead.

h) By bicycle.

Grammar: verb forms

2

What is the correct form of the verbs?

Kate Crawford is Australian, but she (1) *(live)*
___lives___ in England. She (2) *(work)* _____ for
an international bank in London. She (3) *(drive)*
_____ to work in the morning. It (4) *(take)*
_____ her about thirty minutes. The traffic is
very bad in London because thousands of people
(5) *(drive)* _____ to work at the same time.
Kate usually (6) *(get up)* _____ at seven and
(7) *(start)* _____ work at nine. Most of the
people in her bank (8) *(finish)* _____ work at five
but she usually (9) *(finish)* _____ at six or six thirty.

Grammar: questions

3

Choose the correct words for the questions.

1 *Do/Does/Are* pilots earn a good salary?

2 *Do/Does/Are* you speak German?

3 *What/How/Where* do you get to work?

4 *Do/Does/Is* Kate live in Paris?

5 *Do/Does/Are* you understand this exercise?

6 *Where/When/What* do you have for breakfast?

7 *How/How much/How many* do a good pair of shoes cost?

8 *Where/Who/How* does Kate work for?

9 *Do/Does/Are* most people finish work before Kate?

Arranging to meet

4

Tom MacDonald is phoning Kate Crawford. Match Tom's questions (1–7) with Kate's answers (a–g).

1 Hello. Can I speak to Kate Crawford, please? __b__

2 Hello, Kate. This is Tom MacDonald. Do you remember me? ____

3 I'm fine thanks. How are you? ____

4 Can we meet for lunch on Tuesday? ____

5 What time do you usually have lunch? ____

6 Where do you work? ____

7 Do you know a good restaurant near the bank? ____

a) Let me think. Um . . . Yes, there's a nice pizza restaurant called 'Luigi's' in the same street.

b) This is Kate Crawford speaking.

c) In the Anglo-International Bank in Lombard Street.

d) Yes, of course I do. How are you?

e) Let me look in my diary. Yes, that's fine for me.

f) I'm fine, too.

g) At about one o'clock.

Grammar: prepositions

5

Choose the correct word.

1 A: What does Richard Knight do?
   B: He's the director *of/in* Knight and Day.

2 A: Is Kate British?
   B: No, she comes *of/from* Australia.

3 A: Can I speak to Richard Knight, please?
   B: He's *at/on* the phone now. Can you hold the line?

4 A: Does Tom MacDonald travel very much?
   B: Yes, he often goes *at/to* France.

5 A: Does he stay with friends there?
   B: No, he stays *into/in* a hotel.

6 A: Is Tom in France now?
   B: No, he's phoning *from/of* Bristol.

Pronouns: How long does it take you to get to work?

6

Write sentences.

1 Tessa leaves home at seven forty and gets to work at eight thirty.
   It takes her fifty minutes to get to work.

2 Kate leaves home at eight thirty and gets to work at nine o'clock.
   It _____ minutes
   to _____ to work.

3 I leave home at ten to seven and get to work at a quarter past seven.
   It _____
   _____ to work.

4 Two of my friends leave home at eight o'clock and get to the university at half past nine.
   _____
   the university.

5 My friend and I leave home at seven and get to the language school at seven twenty.
   _____
   to the _____ .

Vocabulary: see, hear, talk

Read the letter from Roger and choose the correct verb.

> Dear Tessa,
>
> It is nine o'clock on Sunday morning and I am sitting here in my apartment in San Francisco. The Golden Gate Bridge isn't far away. I can **(1) see/watch** it from my window. I always sit here on Sundays and **(2) hear/listen to** the radio.
>
> San Francisco isn't a very big city but it's very international. You can **(3) hear/listen to** many different languages in the street. Some people **(4) speak/talk** two or three languages. You can **(5) see/watch** foreign language programmes on television.
>
> Why don't you visit me sometime? I'd really like to **(6) see/watch** you again. I often think about you and remember those wonderful days in Cambridge.
>
> Do you remember Ted Stern? He lives here in San Francisco and I **(7) see/watch** him sometimes. We often **(8) speak/talk** about you and our other friends at Cambridge when we were younger.

Vocabulary: opposites

Do you remember the opposites of these words?

go to bed   wrong   finish   before   leave   easy

Correct the mistakes in these sentences.

1 Kate ~~goes to bed~~ at seven o'clock. ___gets up___

2 A: Budapest is the capital of Hungary.

   B: That's *wrong*. _____

3 In England most people *finish* work at nine o'clock in the morning. _____

4 People usually have breakfast *before* they get up in the morning. _____

5 There is a train to London at six o'clock. It takes an hour to get there.

   It *leaves* at seven. _____

6 I don't understand this.

   It's very *easy*. _____

3

Grammar: Present Simple/ Progressive

1

Choose what you can say about the picture: a or b.

1 a) That's Roger. He works in an office.
  b) That's Roger. He is working in an office.

2 a) Roger works at home now.
  b) Roger is working at home now.

3 a) Look at the window. Does it rain?
  b) Look at the window. Is it raining?

4 a) The sun doesn't shine in San Francisco.
  b) The sun isn't shining in San Francisco.

5 a) He talks to Kate.
  b) He is talking to Kate.

6 a) Kate phones from London.
  b) Kate is phoning from London.

7 a) Roger drives to work in his sports car.
  b) Roger is driving to work in his sports car.

8 a) He watches football on TV.
  b) He is watching football on TV.

2

Match the questions (1-7) with the answers (a-g).

1 What does Roger do? _f_

2 What is he doing? _____

3 What does Kate do? _____

4 What is she doing? _____

5 What are you doing? _____

6 What do you do? _____

7 What's your boss doing? _____

a) She's phoning Roger.
b) An exercise in the workbook. Can't you see?
c) I'm a student.
d) He's talking to Kate.
e) She works for Anglo-International Bank.
f) He works for a computer software company.
g) She's working at home today.

3

What's the full question?

1 Roger lives in San Francisco. What about Kate?
  Where does Kate live?

2 I live in a big city. What about you?
  _____ you _____ in a big city?

3 It is raining in San Francisco. What about London?
  _____ it _____ in London?

4 Roger is working today. What about Kate?
  _____ Kate _____ today?

5 I get up at seven in the morning. What about you?
  What time _____ you _____?

6 I understand all the words here. What about you?
  _____ all the words here?

7 It takes me twenty minutes to get to work. What about you?
  How _____ it _____ you
  _____ work?

4

Read the conversation between Kate and Roger. What are the missing words?

Kate: Hello, Roger. This is Kate Crawford.
        I'm (1) <u>ringing</u> from London.

Roger: Kate! (2) _____ are you?

Kate: I'm fine. What about you?

Roger: Oh, not too bad.

Kate: Listen, I'd (3) _____ some information.
        Do you remember Terry Slater?

Roger: Terry Slater? Yes, of course. He works in
        France now.

Kate: Have you (4) _____ his address?

Roger: Just a moment. (5) _____ me look in
        my address book. Yes, I do. (6) _____
        you have a pen?

Kate: Yes. Go on.

Roger: He (7) _____ for a company called
        Poirel International. Rue de Gaulle 24, Paris
        75009.

What's the time?

5

Match the times (1–6) with the clocks and watches (a–f).

1 quarter past nine <u>b</u>   4 twenty past three _____

2 twelve o'clock _____   5 half past seven _____

3 quarter to two _____   6 five to seven _____

Giving directions

6

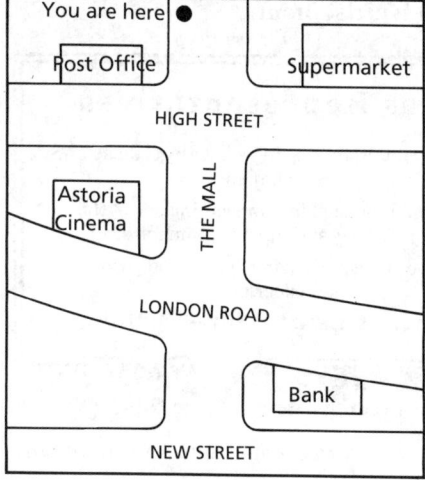

Look at the map and complete the conversations with these sentences.

a) It's just round the corner on the right.
b) Go straight on and take the second street on the right. It's on your right.
c) Yes. Go straight ahead and take the second street on the left.
d) I'm sorry, I don't know. I'm not from here.
e) Yes. Take the first street on the left, and it's on your left.

1 A: Excuse me. Is there a bank near here?
  B: <u>Yes. Go straight ahead and take the</u>
     <u>second street on the left.</u>

2 A: How can I get to the post office, please?
  B: _____
     _____

3 A: Is there a supermarket near here?
  B: _____

4 A: How can I get to the Astoria Cinema, please?
  B: _____
     _____

5 A: Excuse me. How can I get to New Street?
  B: _____
     _____

A job advert

7

Read this advertisement.

Sales Representatives

Do you want an interesting job with good pay and a company car?

Are you interested in representing one of the world's largest computer companies?

Have you got a driving licence and good sales experience?

Contact us at 0800–889900.

Are these sentences true (✓) or false (✗)?

1 A *sales representative* sells things for a company. ✓

2 You can earn good money in this job. ___

3 People with *company cars* can sell them to other people. ___

4 A driving licence isn't necessary for this job. ___

5 We can learn things from our *experience*. ___

6 You can write a letter to this company and get more information. ___

Grammar: negatives

8

Make these sentences true.

1 James has got a wife and two children.
   James hasn't got a wife and two children.

2 Tessa has got a car.
   Tessa hasn't ___ a car.

3 My five-year-old son has got a driving licence.
   Your five-year-old son ___
   a ___ .

4 You've got a British passport.
   I ___ a British passport.

5 You have caviar for breakfast every morning.
   I don't ___ caviar for breakfast every morning.

Vocabulary: money, money, money

9

Use the clues to complete the square. The first letter of each word spells someone's name.

1										
2										
3										
4										
5										

1 Money you give to a waiter, a porter or a taxi driver.(3 letters)
2 If things cost a lot we say they're ___. (9 letters)
3 You can spend money or you can ___ it. (4 letters)
4 A word for money you earn.(6 letters)
5 It's the name of a famous credit card.(15 letters)

Grammar: *Have you got...? / Do you have...?*

10

Which of these examples are American English (A)? Which of them are British English (B)? Which one is British and American (A & B) ?

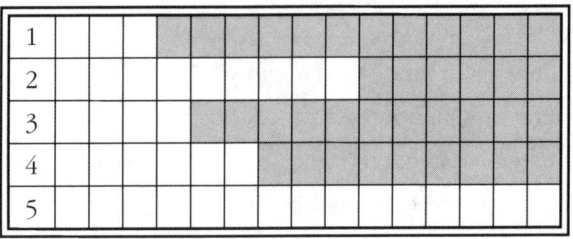

1 Excuse me. Do you have the time? _A_
2 Excuse me. Have you got the time? ___
3 Has Kate got a driving licence? ___
4 Does Roger have a driver's licence? ___
5 I haven't got his address. Have you got it? ___
6 Tessa doesn't have any brothers or sisters. ___
7 I've got a brother but I haven't got a sister. ___
8 I don't have Terry's address. Do you have it? ___
9 Do you have a shower in the morning? ___

4

Conversation management

1

Find good responses for the situation in the picture.

1 A: Do you like champagne?
    B: a) Yes, I like it.
       b) Yes, I do.
       c) Yes, I would. Thank you very much.

2 A: Would you like a glass of champagne?
    B: a) Yes, I like it very much. It is very good.
       b) Yes.
       c) Oh, thank you very much.

3 A: What kind of food would you like to eat?
    B: a) Well, I'm not sure. Can you suggest
          something?
       b) I don't like spaghetti.
       c) I want raw fish.

4 A: Would you like to try the fish?
    B: a) No, you wouldn't.
       b) No, I wouldn't. I don't like fish.
       c) No, not now. Some other time, perhaps.

5 B: Is the fish good here?
    A: a) No, they aren't.
       b) Yes, very.
       c) Fish is very good. You like it.

Grammar: frequency adverbs

2

Match the questions (1–6) with the answers (a–f).

1 How often do you eat foreign food? _c_

2 Do you always get the bus to work? ___

3 Does Tessa ever travel to Spain or France? ___

4 Why doesn't Roger ever travel to Europe? ___

5 How often does Roger eat Japanese food? ___

6 Do you usually get to work before 8 am? ___

a) Yes, I usually get to work at 7.30.

b) No, I sometimes get the train.

c) Rarely. There aren't any good foreign restaurants here.

d) Never. He doesn't like it very much.

e) Yes, she does sometimes.

f) He doesn't have any reason to go there.

Look at Richard Knight's diary.

MON 13th APRIL

10.30 Phone Donald

1.00 Lunch with Jane Sullivan, BBC Radio 4, Mario's Trattoria

7.00 Drinks with Bill Gibson, Hilton Champagne Bar

TUE 14th APRIL

5.30 Check in Heathrow. Flight LH212 Munich

9.00 Arrive Munich

10.30 Meeting TRS

1.30 Lunch with Manfred Kernholz. Münchenhof restaurant

4.30 Check in Munich Airport. Flight LH216 Heathrow

8.30 Phone Donald

WED 15th APRIL

10.00 Phone Donald

12.30 Lunch with Stuart Bell, Holiday Inn

5.30 Cocktail party, Hilton Hotel, Room 540

THUR 16th APRIL

7.00 Check in Heathrow. Flight AF301 Paris

10.30 Arrive Paris

11.30 Meeting with Terry Slater, Poirel International

2.00 Lunch, Restaurant de la Bonne Femme, Rue Rivoli

4.30 Check in Charles De Gaulle Airport. Flight AF314 Heathrow

9.30 Phone Donald

FRI 17th APRIL

8.30 Send fax to Poirel International

1.30 Lunch, Langan's Brasserie

4.00 Phone Donald

6.30 Meet Jack, Olga and Tom in pub near New Era Advertising

SAT 18th APRIL

2.00 Watch rugby on TV (England versus France)

11.30 Phone Donald

SUN 19th APRIL

2.00 Watch football on TV (Manchester Utd–Liverpool)

4.30 'Advertising Today', BBC Radio 4

6.30 Phone Donald

Now circle the right word in the sentences.

1 Richard Knight *never* / (*usually*) gets up very early.
2 He *often* / *rarely* travels to Europe on business.
3 When he's in London he *never* / *always* phones Donald Day to tell him what is happening in the London office.
4 He *rarely* / *always* has lunch in the office.
5 He *rarely* / *often* gets home before 7 pm because he likes to meet friends or business associates for a drink after work.
6 At the weekend he *sometimes* / *never* watches sport on television.
7 He *rarely* / *always* listens to the radio, but this weekend there is a special programme on advertising.

In a restaurant

4

Make questions. Then find answers (a–e) for the questions (1–5).

1 starter you would to like have a

Would you like to have a starter? C

2 you what would like the starter after

3 what like would you steak with your vegetables

4 do what like would after you to dinner

5 sashimi what is

a) It's raw fish or raw seafood.
b) I'd like the fillet steak, please.
c) Perhaps the seafood cocktail.
d) Green beans and carrots.
e) I think I'd like to go to the theatre.

Grammar: *How much/How many*

5

Circle the correct alternative.

1 *How much /How many* peaches would you like?

2 *How much /How many* salad would you like?

3 *How much /How many* cauliflower would you like?

4 *How much /How many* apples would you like?

5 *How much /How many* potatoes would you like?

6 *How much /How many* sugar would you like?

Vocabulary: food

6

What do you know about food? Match the foods (1–12) with the nationalities (a–l).

1 enchiladas __k__   a) Indian
2 paella _____   b) Greek
3 sushi _____   c) English
4 falafel _____   d) Italian
5 moussaka _____   e) French
6 sauerkraut _____   f) Turkish
7 roast beef _____   g) Scottish
8 haggis _____   h) Egyptian
9 croissants _____   i) Japanese
10 spaghetti _____   j) German
11 lamb korma _____   k) Mexican
12 kebabs _____   l) Spanish

Vocabulary: people at work

7

Match the words (1–5) with the definitions (a–e).

1 **passenger** /ˈpæsɪndʒəʳ/*n* __c__

2 **guest** /gest/*n* ____

3 **patient** /ˈpeɪʃənt/*n* ____

4 **customer** /ˈkʌstəməʳ/*n* ____

5 **client** /ˈklaɪənt/*n* ____

a) a person receiving medical treatment
b) a person who pays a professional person or organisation for help or advice
c) a person, not the driver or the crew, travelling in a public or private vehicle
d) someone who buys goods or services from a shop or business regularly
e) a person who is staying in a hotel or guesthouse

Test 1

A Make words from the Review Unit to Unit 4.

1 gnirincsea _increasing_

2 kdes d_____

3 rotcerid d_____

4 wievtnire
   i_____

5 noitresvera
   r_____

6 laess s_____

7 ostfawre s_____

8 tliencs c_____

9 yraid d_____

10 ygance a_____

11 ficeof o_____

12 yralas s_____

13 cesteryra
    s_____

14 eletenohp
    t_____

B Now use some of the words above to complete the sentences.

1 My name's Kate Crawford. I have a
   reservation for a single room with a shower.

2 At Bradford Soft we make computer
   _____

3 I've got an appointment with Richard Knight, but I'm not sure what time. Can you give me my _____?

4 It's on my _____.

5 Knight and Day is an advertising _____.

6 Richard Knight is the _____ of the London _____ of Knight and Day.

7 James Chen has a job _____ at ten o'clock. He wants to ask about the _____.

8 Tessa's _____ is talking to Donald Day on the _____.

C Complete the text.

Kees de Groot is a student. He is (1) ___from___ Rotterdam, but he lives (2) _____ Amsterdam now. He is (3) _____ economics at university there. He (4) _____ near the university in a flat which he shares with three other students. He has classes from two to five in the afternoon and then he usually (5) _____ to the library to study. (6) _____ the evenings he sometimes meets friends in a pub (7) _____ a drink. (8) _____ the weekend he (9) _____ study very much. (10) _____ Saturdays he (11) _____ playing football or squash and he usually goes out with (12) _____ girlfriend on Saturday nights. (13) _____ name is María. She is a Spanish student studying in Amsterdam, too. On Sundays he always (14) _____ very late – about midday. He (15) _____ a big breakfast with cheese, ham and lots of bread and milk. He (16) _____ the radio and reads the newspaper. In the afternoon he studies a bit or (17) _____ sport on television.

D Read this telephone conversation. Circle the correct alternative.

María: Hello. (1) (Is that you)/Are you Kees?

Kees: Yes. Hi, María. (2) *How do you do?/How are you?*

María: Fine, thanks. (3) *What do you do?/What are you doing?*

Kees: Oh, (4) *I'm studying/I study* for an accounting exam. What about you?

María: (5) *I'm finishing/I finish* an assignment for International Relations. Listen. What (6) *you want/do you want* to do on Saturday night?

Kees: (7) *I'm not know/I don't know.* Can you think (8) *of/in* something?

María: Yes. (9) *There's/It's* a good film on at the film club. (10) *Do you like/Would you like* to go?

Kees: (11) *Who's/What's* the name of the film?

María: 'Les Enfants du Paradis'. (12) *There's/It's* an old French film.

Kees: Is it (13) *on/in* French?

María: Yes, it is, but with English subtitles, I think.

Kees: But I don't (14) *talk/speak* French.

María: You (15) *do/can* read the English subtitles.

Kees: OK. What time (16) *is it/does it* start?

María: At 8.30. Do you want (17) *to meet/meet* at the cinema?

Kees: Yes. That's a good idea. What time (18) *do you/would you* like to meet? Eight o'clock?

María: Yes, that's fine. See you then. Bye.

Kees: Bye, María.

Reading

1

Read the text and fill in the gaps with prepositions.

Earth Friendly is a small British company **1** _____with_____ about thirty employees.

The main office and a small factory are about fifteen kilometres
2 _____ Bristol. The company began **3** _____ 1986.
4 _____ that time they made natural shampoos and perfumes
5 _____ women.

At the moment they only sell their products in Britain, but they plan to sell them
6 _____ other parts **7** _____ Europe next year.

Sales are not very good **8** _____ the moment.

Are the statements True (✓) or False (✗)?

1 About thirty people work for Earth Friendly. __✓__
2 The main office is not in the same place as the factory. ____
3 In 1986 the company made cosmetics for men. ____
4 Earth Friendly sells its products all over the world at the moment. ____
5 Sales are not increasing. ____

2

Make questions. Then match the questions (1–6) with the answers (a–f).

1 make does what Earth Friendly
What _does Earth Friendly make_? _b_

a) Near Bristol.

2 a company Earth Friendly very big is
____ Earth Friendly a _____? ____

b) Shampoos and perfume.

3 their main office is where
_____? ____

c) In 1986.

4 the company begin did when
_____? ____

d) Sell their products not only in Britain but in other European countries.

5 sales now very good are
_____? ____

e) No, they aren't.

6 plan what they do to do
_____? ____

f) No. Only about thirty people work there.

Dates

3

Match the words (1–5) with the numbers (a–e).

1 Nineteen eighty–four. __d__

2 The third of June. ____

3 The sixth of March. ____

4 The second of January nineteen ninety-one. ____

5 Two thousand and one. ____

a) 6/3
b) *2001*
c) 2.1.91
d) *1984*
e) *3/6*

Questions

4

Make questions.

1 day today what it is
   What day is it today?

2 make do what they

3 main office where is their located

4 which film you yesterday see did

5 like you too did it

6 was in Lille Tom MacDonald when

7 did Tom MacDonald meet who

Changing arrangements

5

Continue Mr Yamada's sentences with the best alternative.

1 Good morning, Mr Mitchum.
   a) This is Akira Yamada.
   b) I am Akira Yamada.

2 We planned a second meeting.
   a) Why don't you remember?
   b) Perhaps you remember.

3 There is a problem with the date of our next meeting.
   a) That's the reason I phone you.
   b) That's the reason I'm phoning.

4 We would like to meet on the twelfth instead.
   a) Would that be possible?
   b) Please come then.

5 I'm afraid the morning isn't convenient for us.
   a) Is it possible to meet in the afternoon?
   b) Give me another time.

6 At two o'clock?
   a) I don't know. I look in my diary.
   b) Let me look in my diary.

Grammar: present/past

6

Read this letter to Tom from his sister in Canada. Put the verbs into the correct form.

Dear Tom,

How (**1**) (**be**) _____ are _____ you? I hope everything (**2**) (**be**)
_____ fine. It (**3**) (**be**) _____ really nice to talk to you on
the phone last week.

The weather here (**4**) (**be**) _____ very good at the moment, but
last month it (**5**) (**be**) _____ very cold. Yesterday it (**6**) (**begin**)
_____ to rain and now it (**7**) (**be**) _____ warm. I never
(**8**) (**know**) _____ what to wear! I can take the children out to
the park later if it doesn't start to rain again.

Last week Jeff Charlesworth (**9**) (**phone**) _____ me. Do you
remember him? You and he (**10**) (**be**) _____ at school together.
He (**11**) (**be**) _____ married now and has two children. He asked
me to say 'Hello' to you. We arranged to have dinner with Jeff and his
wife next weekend. They (**12**) (**live**) _____ on Maple Drive which is
about two blocks from our house. Jeff and his wife both (**13**) (**get**)
_____ new jobs here so they moved last month from Toronto.
He is in the computer industry and she is a lawyer. It will be interesting
to see them.

Jerry is working very hard at the moment. He (**14**) (**play**) _____
golf every Saturday and squash on Wednesday evenings and he
sometimes (**15**) (**go**) _____ in to the office on Sundays. We don't
see each other very often! He says to say 'Hi' to you too.
Love,
Hilary

Conversation management

1

Kate is talking to a colleague on the telephone. Put her responses in the right order.

a) Thanks very much for calling. Goodbye.
b) Yes. The meeting is on the fourth. Is there a problem?
c) Oh, I see. Let me check my diary. That's OK. I'm free all morning on the seventh.
d) Hello, Daniel. What can I do for you?
e) This is Kate Crawford.
f) Would you like me to call you on the sixth to confirm that?
g) See you on the seventh at 11.30 then.

1 _e_ 2 ___ 3 ___ 4 ___ 5 ___ 6 ___ 7 ___

Question words

2

Complete the questions with *What*, *Where*, *When*, *How*, and *How long*.

1 ___When___ did you get up? — At 5 am!

2 _____ did it take you to get to work? — Four hours!

3 _____ did you do before lunch? — I wrote twenty reports and had five meetings!

4 _____ did you have lunch? — At the Ritz!

5 _____ did you do after lunch? — I answered a few letters and made two phone calls.

6 _____ did you get home? — At midnight!

7 _____ did you feel when you got home? — I felt marvellous!

8 _____ did you go to bed? — At 2 am!

Grammar: comparatives

3

Tessa Saunders and Richard Knight are choosing models for an advertising campaign. Fill each gap with the correct form of the comparative.

Richard: Mark Turnbull was the one with long dark hair.

Tessa: Well, he had (1) (*long*) _____longer_____ hair than the others. I like long hair!

Richard: Mmm. I liked the tall thin chap. Was that Jake Millington?

Tessa: Well, Jake Millington is tall and thin, but Andy Johnson is (2) (*tall*) _____ and (3) (*thin*) _____.

Richard: What's Andy Johnson's fee?

Tessa: About two hundred pounds an hour, I think.

Richard: And Jake Millington?

Tessa: Two hundred and fifty.

Richard: So Millington is (4) (*expensive*) _____. How old is he?

Tessa: He's twenty-six and Andy Johnson is twenty-eight.

Richard: That's too old. I'd like to have someone (5) (*young*) _____. What about Tony Minuto?

Tessa: He's (6) (*old*) _____ than the others, but I think he's (7) (*interesting*) _____.

Richard: Yes, I agree. He's (8) (*good*) _____ for this campaign than the others. But he'll be (9) (*difficult*) _____ to get. He often works abroad.

4

Match the questions (1–5) with the answers (a–e).

1. Are Japanese restaurants more expensive in London than they are in Japan? __b__

2. Was English more important than French in the 1930's? _____

3. Are your English classes now more interesting than the classes you had at school? _____

4. Does Korea manufacture better cars than Germany? _____

5. Are French clothes more elegant than Italian clothes? _____

a) I have no idea. I drive a Renault.

b) I think so. But the food is still delicious.

c) Yes, I think so. At school we didn't practise speaking.

d) Yes, I think so. But I'm French!

e) No, I don't think so. More people studied French then.

Grammar: Past Simple

5

Look at Kate Crawford's diary for yesterday. Complete sentences about the things she did.

MONDAY 20th APRIL

9.00 Phone Francesca Di Pietro.

9.30 Finish translation of documents for
      Poirel International.

10.30 Explain technical problems to Susan.

12.00 Go to dentist.

1.00 Have lunch with Marie.

2.30 Discuss translation problems with
      Matthew.

4.00 Correct mistakes in French – English
      translation in the new brochures.

5.00 Leave work early!

1 ____She phoned Francesca Di Pietro.____

2 _____ the translation of the
documents for Poirel International.

3 _____ some technical
_____ to Susan.

4 _____ the dentist.

5 _____ lunch _____ .

6 _____ some translation
problems with _____ .

7 _____ the mistakes in the
_____
_____ .

8 _____ .

Vocabulary: 'in between' words

6

Use these words to complete this description of Mr Average: *average, middle-aged, centre, middle, in between.*

Mr Average isn't tall or short. He's (1) __in between__ . How old is he? About 42, I think. Not very young and not very old – (2) '_____' would be a good description. I mean that he's not at the beginning of life and he's not at the end. He's in the (3) _____ . His political opinions aren't really left or right. Perhaps we can say he votes for the (4) _____ parties. He isn't very intelligent, but you can't say he's stupid. He's just like his name: Mr (5) '_____'.

7

Travel arrangements

1

Read this conversation between a clerk in a travel agency and a customer. Look at what the clerk says (1–6). Put the customer's part (a–f) in the right order.

1 Good afternoon. Universal Travel. Can I help you?

2 I see. When do you want to travel?

3 In the morning or in the afternoon?

4 There's an Alitalia flight from Heathrow at six twenty-five in the morning.

5 At eight fifty. That's local time – an hour ahead of us.

6 There's a flight from Rome to London at seven twenty in the evening, that arrives in London at five to nine.

a) OK. I'd like one seat on that flight, please, in business class. When's the last flight from Rome to London the same day? _____

b) What time does it arrive in Rome? _____

c) On 6th June. _____

d) In the morning. I have a meeting in Rome at 12.00. _____

e) Yes. I'd like to inquire about flights to Rome. __1__

f) Good. I'll come back on that flight. _____

Now find the mistakes in this document.

Universal Travel

Your travel details

Mr Thomas Dietz

Invoice Number 156
Your Contact: Sam

From: London Heathrow
To: Rome Leonardo da Vinci
Depart 6 (July) 06.45
Arrive 08.15

Return 7 July 20.00
Arrive London 23.10

Class: Economy

Comparing people

2

Study the information about María Pérez and Kate Crawford. Write sentences comparing them.

MARIA PEREZ	KATE CRAWFORD
• gets up at 8 or 9	• gets up at 7
• has breakfast between 8.30 and 9.30	• has breakfast at 7.15
• has lunch at 12.30	• has lunch between 1 and 2
• gets about six hours sleep	• gets about seven hours sleep
• spends about £80 a week	• spends about £100 a week
• went abroad for the first time last year	• often travels to Germany and France
• is 22 years old	• is 27 years old

1 María gets up later than Kate.

2 María has breakfast _____ than Kate.

3 Kate has lunch _____

_____ .

4 María gets _____ Kate.

5 Kate spends _____

_____ .

6 Kate travels _____ .

7 María is _____ .

Vocabulary: air travel

3

Look at the international departures and arrivals boards and write the correct flight numbers.

ARRIVALS

		Expected	
GR2	Melbourne	Cancelled	
QF2	Singapore	23.00	Landed
CP3	Hong Kong	23.00	Landed
AC1	Beijing	23.30	Delayed
KL3	Colombo	23.45	Landed
GU1	Jakarta	00.10	
SA4	Perth	02.45	

DEPARTURES

KL2	Kuala Lumpur	17.00	Delayed
GU2	Jakarta	19.00	Delayed
AC3	Canton	20.00	Boarding Gate 46
AC2	Beijing	20.00	Cancelled
CP3	Hong Kong	20.20	Boarding Gate 53
QF1	Sydney	21.00	Wait in lounge
SA3	Perth	22.00	Wait in lounge

1 Find a flight from Singapore. __QF2__

2 Find a flight that is going to be late. _____

3 Find a flight boarding at gate 46. _____

4 Find a flight that isn't leaving. _____

5 Find a flight that arrives at a quarter to three. _____

4 Read these airport announcements.

'Passengers for flight IB 714 to Madrid can now check in at desk D. Passengers can take only one piece of hand luggage on board the aircraft.'

'This is an important announcement for all passengers. Please keep your luggage with you at all times. Do not leave your luggage unattended at any time.'

'Would Miss K Crawford, a passenger arriving on Air France flight 309 from Paris, please contact Airport Information?'

'Would Herr Kernholz, last remaining passenger on Lufthansa flight 214 to Frankfurt, please go immediately to gate 35?'

'First and final call for passengers on KLM flight 409 to Colombo. Now boarding at gate 25.'

'British Airways apologise for the delay to passengers on flight BA 214. Please wait in the lounge and listen for further announcements.'

Are these statements true (✓) or false (✗)?

1 Herr Kernholz is late for his flight. ___✓___

2 There is a message for Kate Crawford. _____

3 You can put your bags anywhere and go to the bar. _____

4 The KLM flight leaves before the British Airways flight. _____

5 You can take a big suitcase onto the plane to Madrid. _____

Grammar: prepositions

5

Complete the letter with the missing prepositions.

Catalaco SA

Marc Braun
Director
Catalaco SA
Terry Slater   Diagonal 105
Marketing Manager   60009 Barcelona
Poirel International Ltd
Rue de Gaulle 24   5 May
Paris 75009

RE: My visit to Paris next week

Dear Terry,

I am writing to confirm my travel details for next week. I leave Barcelona on Iberia flight IB 310. It departs (1) __from__ Barcelona (2) _____ 10.50 am next Friday and arrives (3) _____ Paris (4) ____ 11.20.

Our meeting is at 2.30. Is there a bus or a metro that goes (5) _____ the airport (6) ____ the centre of the city? I can get a taxi (7) _____ the hotel and meet you in head office (8) _____ 12.30.

My return flight leaves (9) _____ 8.30 pm. I don't want to get (10) _____ the airport any later than 7.00. I'd like to write the report on our meeting when I get there. My boss wants me to finish it before I land (11) _____ Barcelona airport!

Looking forward to seeing you (12) _____ the fifteenth.

Best wishes,

Marc Braun

Marc Braun

Times and dates

6

Write these times and years in words.

1 7.00 ___Seven o'clock_____

2 11.00 _____

3 1989 _____

4 3.15 _____

5 4.30 _____

6 1945 _____

Questions and answers

7

Match the questions (1–5) with the answers (a–e).

1 (Are you sure you wouldn't like a little glass of champagne? _d_

2 (Was the room empty when you looked in?__

3 (Can you pay for my sandwich? I haven't got my wallet with me. __

4 (Can I help you with that letter?__

5 (Can we meet on Tuesday?__

a) (I'm afraid I haven't any time free at all then. Can you suggest another day?

b) (No. There were some people standing near the window.

c) (Yes, please. There are some words I don't understand.

d) (No, thank you. I don't want any more to drink. I'm driving.

e) (I'm sorry but I haven't got any more money.

When you were younger

1

Look at Terry Slater's curriculum vitae.

CURRICULUM VITAE

Name: Terence Simon Slater

Date of Birth: 5/9/63

Place of Birth: Manchester, UK

Education: William Dean Primary School, Manchester (1968–74); Ignacious Loyola Boys' College, Manchester (1974–81); University of Cambridge 1981–84

Educational Qualifications: B.A. (French and Italian)

Positions held
1984–86: Teacher of English, Academia Shelley, Arezzo, Italy
1986–89: Director of Studies, Speed School of English, Oxford, UK
1989–92: Marketing Director, Lingua Tours International, UK
1992–   Marketing Director, Poirel International, France

Personal Details
Married Margaret McLeod 1988
Two children: Sophia (born 1989), William (born 1991)

Correct these false statements about Terry.

1 Terry was born in nineteen thirty-six.
   He wasn't born in nineteen thirty-six.
   He was born in nineteen sixty-three.

2 Terry went to primary school in Cambridge.
   He didn't _____ in Cambridge. He _____ to primary school in Manchester.

3 He went to Oxford University.
   He _____ to Oxford University.
   He _____ to Cambridge University.

4 He studied German and Russian.
   He _____ German and Russian.
   He _____ French and Italian.

5 He taught English in Spain.
   _____ English in _____.
   He _____.

6 He came back to England in 1985.
   He _____ to England in 1985. He _____ back _____ 1986.

7 He taught French and Italian in Oxford.
   He _____ French and Italian there. He _____ English.

8 His son, William, was born in 1989.
   William _____ in 1989.
   _____ in 1991.

Key

Review unit

1 2 e 3 c 4 a 5 f 6 b

2 2 a 3 a 4 b 5 c 6 b 7 b 8 b

3 2 e 3 a 4 f 5 b 6 d

4 2 one fifty-nine 3 seven oh four 4 twelve oh three 5 fourteen seventy-seven 6 four oh nine

5 2 What is she wearing? 3 Who is she? 4 Where does she live? 5 How old is she? 2 (She is wearing) a suit. 3 Tessa Saunders. 4 (She lives in) London. 5 (She is) twenty-nine.

6 2 at 3 from 4 in 5 in 6 on 7 near

7 2 No 3 I don't know 4 No 5 Yes 6 Yes 7 Yes 8 I don't know 9 Yes

8 2 Her 3 She 4 He 5 His 6 Her 7 He 8 He 9 She

11 2 Can you play tennis? 3 Where are you from? 4 How old are you? 5 What do you do?

12 2 h 3 b 4 e 5 c 6 d 7 a 8 g

13 2 jacket 3 one 4 house 5 water

14

C H I N E S E			I		H I S			

(crossword grid)

Unit 1

1 2 b 3 a 4 b 5 a 6 c

2 2 Is English easy? 3 Where are you from? 4 Can you speak English? 5 Can I help you? 6 Where are you staying?

3 2 ~~not~~ first 3 ~~light~~ heavy 4 ~~bad~~ good

4 2 ~~Their~~ Her 3 ~~He~~ She 4 ~~He~~ It 5 ~~them~~ him

5 2 Can 3 Where am 4 Do you 5 first visit 6 How long

6 2 How many 3 How many 4 How much 5 How much 6 How much 7 How many

7 2 her 3 her 4 our 5 them 6 they 7 them 8 us 9 it 10 me

8 2 What 3 How

9 2 blouse 3 shirt 4 tights 5 tie 6 suit 7 dress 8 trousers 9 coat 10 suit 11 jacket

10

	Men	Women
suit	✓	✓
dress		✓
trousers	✓	✓
tie	✓	
shirt	✓	✓
skirt		✓
coat	✓	✓
blouse		✓
jacket	✓	✓
tights		✓

11 2 jeans 3 raincoat 4 hat 5 jacket

12 2 looking 3 Have 4 size 5 size 6 me 7 much 8 it

Unit 2

1 2 c 3 h 4 e 5 a 6 f 7 b 8 d

2 2 works 3 drives 4 takes 5 drive 6 gets up 7 starts 8 finish 9 finishes

3 2 Do 3 How 4 Does 5 Do 6 What 7 How much 8 Who 9 Do

4 2 d 3 f 4 e 5 g 6 c 7 a

5 2 from 3 on 4 to 5 in 6 from

6 2 takes her thirty/get 3 takes me twenty-five minutes/get 4 It takes them an hour and a half to get to 5 It takes us twenty minutes to get/language school

7 2 listen to 3 hear 4 speak 5 watch 6 see 7 see 8 talk

8 2 right 3 start 4 after 5 arrives 6 difficult

Unit 3

1 2 b 3 b 4 b 5 b 6 b 7 a 8 a

2 2 d 3 e 4 a 5 b 6 c 7 g

3 2 Do/live 3 Is/raining 4 What is/doing 5 do/get up 6 Do you understand 7 long does/take/to get to

4 2 How 3 like 4 got 5 Let 6 Do 7 works

5 2 d 3 a 4 c 5 e 6 f

6 2 a 3 e 4 b 5 d

7 2 ✓ 3 ✗ 4 ✗ 5 ✓ 6 ✓

8 2 got 3 hasn't got/driving licence 4 haven't got 5 have

9

1	T	I	P						
2	E	X	P	E	N	S	I	V	E
3	S	A	V	E					
4	S	A	L	A	R	Y			
5	A	M	E	R	I	C	A	N	E X P R E S S

10 2 B 3 B 4 A 5 B 6 A 7 B 8 A 9 A & B

Unit 4

1 2 c 3 a 4 c 5 b

2 2 b 3 e 4 f 5 d 6 a

3 2 often 3 always 4 rarely 5 rarely 6 sometimes
7 rarely

4 2 What would you like after the starter? 3 What
vegetables would you like with your steak? 4 What
would you like to do after dinner? 5 What is
sashimi? 2 b 3 d 4 e 5 a

5 2 How much 3 How much 4 How many 5 How
many 6 How much

6 2 l 3 i 4 h 5 b 6 j 7 c 8 g 9 e 10 d 11 a 12 f

7 2 e 3 a 4 d 5 b

Test 1

A 2 desk 3 director 4 interview 5 reservation
6 sales 7 software 8 clients 9 diary 10 agency
11 office 12 salary 13 secretary 14 telephone

B 1 reservation 2 software 3 diary 4 desk
5 agency 6 director/office 7 interview/salary
8 secretary/ telephone

C 2 in 3 studying 4 lives 5 goes 6 In 7 for 8 At
9 doesn't 10 On 11 likes 12 his 13 Her
14 gets up 15 has 16 listens to 17 watches

D 2 How are you? 3 What are you doing? 4 I'm
studying 5 I'm finishing 6 do you want 7 I don't
know 8 of 9 There's 10 Would you like
11 What's 12 It's 13 in 14 speak 15 can
16 does it 17 to meet 18 would you

Unit 5

1 2 from 3 in 4 At 5 for 6 in 7 of 8 at 2 ✗
3 ✗ 4 ✓ 5 ✓

2 2 Is/very big company? 3 Where is their main office?
4 When did the company begin? 5 Are sales very
good now? 6 What do they plan to do? 2 f 3 a
4 c 5 e 6 d

3 2 e 3 a 4 c 5 b

4 2 What do they make? 3 Where is their main office
located? 4 Which film did you see yesterday? 5 Did
you like it too? 6 When was Tom MacDonald in
Lille? 7 Who did Tom MacDonald meet?

5 2 b 3 b 4 a 5 a 6 b

6 2 is 3 was 4 is 5 was 6 began 7 is 8 know
9 phoned 10 were 11 is 12 live 13 got
14 plays 15 goes

Unit 6

1 2 d 3 b 4 c 5 f 6 g 7 a

2 2 How long 3 What 4 Where 5 What 6 When
7 How 8 When

3 2 taller 3 thinner 4 more expensive 5 younger
6 older 7 more interesting 8 better 9 more
difficult

4 2 e 3 c 4 a 5 d

5 2 She finished 3 She explained/problems 4 She
went to 5 She had/with Marie. 6 She
discussed/Matthew. 7 She corrected/French-English
translation. 8 She left work early.

6 2 middle-aged 3 middle 4 centre 5 Average

Unit 7

1 2 c 3 d 4 b 5 a 6 f ~~06.45~~ 06.25 ~~08.15~~ 08.50
~~July~~ 6 June ~~20.10~~ 19.20 ~~22.10~~ 20.55
~~Economy~~ Business

2 2 later 3 later than María 4 less sleep than
5 more money than María 6 abroad more often
than María 7 younger than Kate

3 2 AC1 3 AC3 4 AC2 5 SA4

4 2 ✓ 3 ✗ 4 ✓ 5 ✗

5 2 at 3 in 4 at 5 from 6 to 7 from 8 at 9 at
10 to 11 at 12 on

6 2 Eleven o'clock 3 Nineteen eighty-nine 4 Quarter
past three 5 Half past four 6 Nineteen forty-five

7 2 b 3 e 4 c 5 a

Unit 8

1 2 go to primary school/went 3 didn't go/went
4 didn't study/studied 5 He didn't
teach/Spain/taught English in Italy. 6 didn't come
back/came/in 7 didn't teach/taught 8 wasn't
born/He was born

2 2 get 3 gets 4 played 5 discusses 6 discussed
7 go 8 went 9 grow up 10 grows up 11 thinks
12 thought 13 design 14 designs

3 2 Did/did you 3 Did/does 4 Did you/did you study
5 Did you/did you see 6 Did you/did you live

4 2 Do you like sushi? 3 Excuse me for asking, but
are you married? 4 Are you Italian? 5 Did you go
to university? 6 What did you do last weekend?
7 Did you come here in a car? 2 d 3 c 4 a 5 e
6 g 7 b

5 2 I didn't 3 am 4 I do 5 I can 6 No, I don't
7 No, I didn't.

6 2 have 3 become 4 get 5 get 6 get 7 have

Test 2

A 2 c 3 b 4 b 5 c 6 b 7 a 8 a 9 b 10 c
11 b 12 c 13 a 14 a 15 b 16 c 17 a

B 2 is shining 3 are 4 are drinking 5 are staying
6 have 7 eat 8 go 9 are 10 met 11 spoke
12 began 13 was 14 went 15 had

Unit 9

1 2 a 3 a 4 b 5 b 6 a 7 a 8 b 9 b 10 a 11 a
12 b 13 b 14 a

2 2 For one day 3 ago 4 For two 5 days ago
6 For two days

3 2 For six years. 3 Two years ago. 4 For three
years. 5 Nine years ago. 6 Eighteen years ago.
7 Nineteen years ago. 8 For eleven years.

4 2 shouldn't translate 3 I should learn 4 I
should/in English 5 I shouldn't think/speak English
6 I should buy 7 I should read English books, too
8 I shouldn't stop when I see a word I don't
understand.

5 2 told 3 said 4 said 5 told 6 told

6 2 public 3 glad 4 rude

7 2 happy 3 sad 4 lucky 5 sad 6 unlucky 7 sorry
8 glad 9 lucky

Unit 10

1 2 a 3 b 4 a 5 a 6 b 7 a ~~Howatt~~ Mellor
~~Mellor~~ Howatt ~~last week~~ next month
~~(241) 369 575~~ (224) 639 757

2 2 d 3 e 4 c 5 a

3 2 Could you translate these letters into French
before tomorrow? 3 Could you speak English three
years ago? 4 Could you tell me something about
the job? 5 Could you type these letters for me?
6 Could you type five years ago? 7 Could I speak to
Mr Knight, please? 2 R 4 R 5 R 7 R

4 2 trips 3 journeys 4 flights 5 cruises 6 go on
7 take

5 2 a 3 a+c 4 a+b 5 c 6 c 7 c 8 b 9 b+c
10 a+b 11 a+b

6 2 will be 3 won't be 4 am 5 will be 6 go
7 will stay 8 will meet 9 will be

7 2 confused 3 excited 5 tiring 7 bored
8 exciting 9 satisfied

Unit 11

1 2 ~~heaviest~~ lightest ~~largest~~ smallest
~~most expensive~~ cheapest ~~worst~~ best

2 2 the biggest 3 the most intelligent 4 the most
expensive 5 the most common 6 the highest
7 the most popular

3 2 fast 3 good 4 quickly 5 sucessfully 6 quiet
7 badly 2 immediately 3 successful 4 quickly/well
5 bad

4

	have	take	go on
1 a bath or shower	✓	✓	
2 a taxi		✓	
3 a seat	✓	✓	
4 an aspirin	✓	✓	
5 a message		✓	
6 an exam		✓	
7 a coffee	✓		
8 a flight		✓	✓
9 a good time	✓		
10 your time		✓	
11 a journey		✓	✓

5 2 c 3 b 4 c 5 a 6 a

6 2 b 3 d 4 a 5 c 6 f

7 (credit card) ~~leather~~ (tights) ~~wool~~ (sofa) ~~paper~~
(ladder) ~~nylon~~ (jacket) ~~platinum~~ (raincoat) ~~suede~~
(serviette) ~~leather~~

Unit 12

1 2 b 3 b 4 c 5 b 6 a

2 2 has to 3 has to 4 can 5 has to 6 has to
7 can 8 will 9 have to

3 2 anything 3 something 4 nothing 5 something
6 Nothing 7 something 8 anything

4 2 Why doesn't the printer work? 3 Would you like
anything to drink? 4 What would you like for your
birthday? 5 What would you like for breakfast? 2 b
3 a 4 e 5 c

5 2 pleased 3 afraid 4 depressed 5 hopeful
6 worried 7 disappointed 8 relaxed

6 2 tall 3 tall 4 tall

Test 3

A 2 a 3 b 4 a 5 c 6 a 7 b 8 c 9 a 10 b
11 a 12 c 13 c 14 c 15 a 16 b 17 b 18 c
19 a 20 a 21 c 22 a 23 b 24 c 25 a

Unit 13

1 2 ✗ 3 ✗ 4 ✗ 5 ✓ 6 ✓ 7 ✓ 8 ✗

2 2 earn 3 borrow 4 lend 5 cost 6 pay 7 spend

3 2 b 3 b 4 a

4 2 a+b 3 a+b 4 b+c 5 a+c 6 a+b 7 b+c
8 a+c

5 2 Tom is going to save/a new car 3 Tom is going to
buy some new 4 Tom is going to drink 5 Tom is
going to eat 6 Tom is going to lose some 7 Tom
is going to live/life

6 2 ✓ 3 ✓ 4 ✓ 5 ✗ 6 ✓ 2 rise 3 increase/raise
4 rise/increase 5 rise/increase 6 raise/increase
7 raise 8 increase

Unit 14

1 2 e 3 d 4 c 5 h 6 i 7 g 8 a 9 b

2 2 c 3 b 4 b 5 b 6 b

3 2 working 3 was 4 been 5 was 6 living 7 got
8 worked 9 was

4 2 translate 3 connection 4 apply 5 argument 6
invest 7 advertisement 8 employ 9 interview 2
translate 3 connection 4 apply
5 arguments 6 invest 7 advertisements
8 employs 9 interview

5 2 ✗ 3 ✗ 4 ✗ 5 ✗ 6 ✗ 7 ✗ 8 ✗ 9 ✓
2 advise 3 include 4 enclose 5 salary 6 any
7 any 8 Someone

6 2 which 3 who 4 which 5 who 6 who

Unit 15

1 2 b 3 a 4 c 5 a

2 2 eats 3 are 4 was 5 study 6 tells 7 told
8 told 9 read 10 reads 11 reading 12 read
13 drive 14 drives 15 drove 16 driving
17 sees 18 saw 19 seeing 20 seen

3 4 No, yesterday I (read) *The Daily Telegraph*.

4 2 ✓ 3 ✓ 4 ✗ 5 ✓ 6 ✓ 7 ✗ 8 ✓

5 2 read 3 do 4 done 5 were 6 been 7 studied
8 studied 9 told 10 told 11 driving 12 driven
13 saw 14 seen

6 2 Have you done this kind of exercise 3 Have you
been waiting 4 Should I wear a suit to the 5 Is the
company doing well 6 Does this company pay its
employees 7 Have you ever eaten sashimi 2 f
3 a 4 g 5 b 6 c 7 e

7 2 tell 3 said 4 told 5 made 6 making 7 done
8 told 9 said

Unit 16

1 2 a 3 b 4 b 5 a 6 a 7 a 8 a 9 a

2 2 met/ hasn't 3 met before/haven't we 4 can meet
him/can't you 5 's studied/before, hasn't he
6 met you at/party, didn't I 7 study English at the
language school on the corner, don't you 8 've
visited England before, haven't they

3 2 has 3 has 4 is 5 has 6 is 7 has 8 is

4 2 ago 3 get 4 yet 5 was 6 come 7 have
8 haven't 9 do 10 would 11 have 12 will
13 going to 14 phone 15 looking

5 2 e 3 a 4 g 5 b 6 c 7 d

6 2 ✓ 3 ✓ 4 ✗ 5 ✓ 6 ✗ 7 ✓ 8 ✓ 9 ✗ 10 ✓
11 ✗ 12 ✓ 13 ✓ 14 ✗ 4 met Tom for the first
time in April this year 6 speaks French well, doesn't
she? 9 long have you known Kate? 11 price of
living is higher than it was last year. 14 This is/I've
driven this car.

Test 4

A 2 a 3 c 4 a 5 b 6 c 7 a 8 b 9 b 10 c 11 a
12 b 13 c 14 b 15 a

B 2 has 3 seem 4 interviewed 5 ago 6 fall 7 has
8 plans 9 there 10 more

·Verb forms

2

Complete the table.

Present	Past
answer/answers	1 answered
2 3	got
play/plays	4
discuss/5	6
7 /goes	8
9 /10	grew up
think/11	12
13 /14	designed

Grammar: short questions to show interest

3

Complete these conversations.

1 A: I had a dog when I was a child.
   B: _Did_ you? What _did you_ call it?

2 A: I had a wonderful weekend.
   B: _____ you? Where _____ go?

3 A: I visited my uncle in Australia.
   B: _____ you? Where _____ he live in
   Australia?

4 A: I studied modern languages at university.
   B: _____? Which modern languages
   _____?

5 A: I went to the cinema last night.
   B: _____? Which film _____?

6 A: I lived in Japan when I was younger.
   B: _____? How long _____
   _____ there?

Questions and answers

4

Make questions. Then match the questions (1–7) with the answers (a–g).

1 your is first this to visit London
   Is this your first visit to London?   _f_

2 you sushi like do
   _____ _____

3 me excuse asking for, are but married you
   _____ _____

   _____ _____

4 Italian you are
   _____ _____

5 you did university go to
   _____ _____

   _____ _____

6 you last weekend did do what
   _____ _____

   _____ _____

7 come you in a did here car
   _____ _____

   _____ _____

a) No, I'm not. I'm Swiss, but I speak Italian
   fluently.
b) Yes, I did. My boyfriend drove me here in his
   new Porsche.
c) Yes, I am. That's my wife over there near the
   door.
d) I don't know very much about Japanese food.
   What is it?
e) Yes, I did. I studied economics at the University
   if Amsterdam.
f) Yes, it is. I think it's a very interesting city.
g) Not very much. I saw a film and met some
   friends. What about you?

Grammar: short answers

5

Make short answers for these questions.

1 (Excuse me. Are you an American?)   <u>No, I'm not.</u>

2 (Did you speak English when you were a child?)   No, _____.

3 (Are you studying English?)   Yes, I _____.

4 (Do you usually have lunch before four o'clock?)   Yes, _____.

5 (Can you ride a bicycle?)   Yes, _____.

6 (Do you usually have a glass of champagne with breakfast?)   ____, _____.

7 (Did you have champagne and caviar for breakfast yesterday?)   _____.

Vocabulary: get/have/become

6

Complete these sentences with the correct verb: *get*, *have* or *become*.

1 Where can I __*get*__ a good dictionary?

2 Do you usually _____ lunch in a restaurant?

3 My son wants to _____ a doctor when he is older.

4 It's very difficult to _____ a job at the moment.

5 Does it usually _____ very cold in December?

6 You can _____ a bus or you can take a taxi.

7 Do you often _____ arguments with your friends?

Test 2

A   Find the correct alternative.

1   The company plans to sell its products in
    Asia ____.
    a) next year   b) last year   c) in 1987

2   Kate's mother never buys clothes from shops.
    She ____ them at home.
    a) does   b) manufactures   c) makes

3   I'm afraid 10th February isn't very ____ for me.
    a) busy   b) convenient   c) well

4   I got ____ at midnight.
    a) at home   b) home   c) in home

5   People here usually ____ coffee at about ten
    o'clock.
    a) has   b) takes   c) have

6   I ____ the evening with some Italian friends
    last Friday.
    a) passed   b) spent   c) had

7   I had a headache, so I took an aspirin. I feel
    much ____ now.
    a) better   b) well   c) good

8   Can I ____ you a few questions?
    a) make   b) do   c) ask

9   Most women are ____ than their husbands.
    a) more young   b) younger   c) young

10 ____ you like to pay for the ticket by cheque or
    credit card?
    a) Do   b) Are   c) Would

11 She didn't give me ____ information about the
    meeting.
    a) many   b) much   c) less

12 The passengers got into the plane. Then they
    ____.
    a) landed   b) arrived   c) took off

13 Excuse me, Barbara. I'd like you to meet a
    friend from New York. ____ Ken Augstein.
    a) This is   b) It is   c) That is

14 I think I ____ what the problem is.
    a) see   b) hear   c) look

15 Look! The bus ____.
    a) comes   b) is coming   c) came

16 My boss ____ in Canada.
    a) born   b) is born   c) was born

17 Where ____ grow up?
    a) did you   b) are you   c) do you

B   Read this letter from María in France to Kees in Spain and put the verbs into the correct form..

Dear Kees,

The weather here in Brittany (1) (**be**) __is__
perfect. The sun (2) (**shine**) _____ and
the beaches here (3) (**be**) _____ wonderful. Janet
and I (4) (**drink**) _____ some beer in a
cafe at the moment. We (5) (**stay**) _____ at a
small hotel here in Dinan. We usually (6) (**have**)
_____ breakfast there and then (7) (**eat**)
_____ lunch in a small restaurant. In the evenings
we often (8) (**go**) _____ to the same restaurant
for dinner.

There (9) (**be**) _____ people from all over the
world here. Yesterday evening we (10) (**meet**)
_____ two Japanese girls. At first we (11) (**speak**)
_____ to them in French but then we
(12) (**begin**) _____ to speak English. That
(13) (**be**) _____ far easier for them.

Last Tuesday we (14) (**go**) _____ to
the city of Saint Malo. We (15) (**have**) _____ a
wonderful time there, too.

I miss you, but not too much. Write back soon!
Love,
María.

9

Formal or informal?

1

Which sentences do you
a) use with friends?
b) use with people you don't know very well?
Mark the sentences a or b.

1 (Good morning. Could you tell me
where the manager's office is? __b__

2 (Hi. How's life? _____

3 (Have a great trip!
Take care! _____

4 (I hope you have a pleasant
journey. Goodbye. _____

5 (Excuse me. Is it possible to
make a phone call? _____

6 (Can I use your phone
for a minute? _____

7 (How are things? _____

8 (How do you do? _____

9 (Pleased to meet you. _____

10 (See you later!
Have a nice day! _____

11 (*Write back soon.* _____

12 (I look forward to receiving
your reply. ___

13 (Yours sincerely, Marc Braun. _____

14 (*Love, María.* _____

Grammar: for/ago

2

Tessa's week

Sunday	– Today I am in London
Saturday	– got back to London at 9 pm
Friday	– Munich
Thursday	– Munich
Wednesday	– Madrid
Tuesday	– Paris
Monday	– left for Paris at 8 am

It is Sunday today and Tessa is at home in
London. Look at the table and then answer
these questions. Use only three words in
your answers: *For ... days* or *... days ago.*

1 When was she in Madrid? ___Four___ days ago.

2 How long was she there? _____ _____ _____.

3 When did she go to Paris? Six days _____.

4 How long did she stay there? _____ _____ days.

5 When did she go to Munich? Three _____ _____.

6 How long did she stay there? _____ _____ _____.

3

Read this information about David Kale. Then answer each question about him in only three words: *For ... years* or *... years ago*.

David Kale

(30)	Age now
(28)	Left Orway Foods and began working for Artaud International
(22)	Began working for Orway Foods
(21)	Finished his studies at London University
(18)	Began his studies at London University
(12)	Started school in Britain
(11)	Left India with his parents and emigrated to Britain

1 When did he leave Orway Foods?
   Two years ago

2 How long did he work there?
   _____

3 When did he start working for Artaud International?
   _____

4 How long did he study at London University?
   _____

5 When did he finish his studies there?
   _____

6 When did he start school in Britain?
   _____

7 When did he leave India?
   _____

8 How long did David live in India?
   _____

Grammar: *should/shouldn't*

4

Here is some advice about learning English.

Now make sentences about what you should and shouldn't do.

1 I __should buy__ a good English-only dictionary.

2 I _____ every new word I learn.

3 _____ words in complete sentences.

4 _____ try to think _____.

5 _____ in my own language when I _____.

6 _____ English-language newspapers.

7 _____.

8 _____.

Vocabulary: *say* and *tell*

5

Here is part of a letter to Kate. Choose the best word.

*I want to apply for a transfer to head office, so I asked my boss what I should do. He (1)(**said**)/**told** that it's a good idea to talk to the people in head office and find out about vacancies. I phoned a friend there and she (2) **said**/**told** me that someone in her section is leaving next month. She (3) **said**/**told** that the job is similar, so it wouldn't be too difficult for me. I asked about the boss of the section and my friend (4) **said**/**told** that she's very nice and very efficient. She (5) **said**/**told** me that I should phone again next week to speak to the boss. When I (6) **said**/**told** my boss about the phone call, he was pleased for me, but sorry I planned to leave.*

Word families

6

Find the word that doesn't belong.

1 suggestion   opinion   idea   (advise)
2 confidential   private   public   secret
3 glad   enjoy   like   admire
4 polite   kind   helpful   rude

Vocabulary: feelings

7

Study the definitions. Then circle the correct alternative.

glad /glæd/*adj* [never before a noun] pleased and happy: *I'm glad he's got the job.*| *I'm glad* **about** *her promotion.*| *We were so glad to hear that your daughter's recovered from her illness.*

hap·py /'hæpi/*adj* **1** feeling, expressing, or giving pleasure and satisfaction: *a happy child* | *you look very happy.* | *a happy marriage* | *I'm not very happy about their decision.* –opposite **unhappy**

luck·y /'lʌki/*adj* having, resulting from, or bringing good luck: *He's a lucky man.* | *That was a lucky find!* | *I carry a lucky charm to protect me when I travel.* –opposite **unlucky**

sor·ry /'sɒri ‖ 'sɑːri, 'sɔːri/ *adj* [never before a noun] sad: *I'm so sorry* **about** *your husband's death.* | *He was sorry to hear the news of the accident.* | *I'm sorry to have to tell you this.*

1 It was a very *glad*/(*sad*) day for our team.
2 Tessa wasn't very *happy*/*glad* when she worked for Bell and Winter.
3 The film had a very *sad*/*unlucky* ending.
4 It was *happy*/*lucky* she remembered to telephone the airport. The flight was delayed.
5 He told me a very *sad*/*sorry* story about his parents.
6 People say it's *sad*/*unlucky* to walk under a ladder.
7 A: You're standing on my foot!
   B: Oh, I am *sorry*/*sad*.
8 He was really *glad*/*lucky* to see me. I could tell by the smile on his face.
9 Today is my *happy*/*lucky* day. I won the lottery!

Taking a message

1

Read this dialogue. Find the polite response for the receptionist: a or b.

1 Good morning. This is Jack Mellor. I'm from Howatt International. I'd like to speak to Miriam Feldman, please.

a) She's not here. Call later, not now.
b) I'm afraid she's not available at the moment.

2 Oh, could I leave a message for her?

a) Yes, of course.
b) All right, leave your message.

3 It's about her visit to our factory in Scotland. When would she like to come?

a) You are speaking too fast. I don't understand you.
b) Could you speak a little more slowly, please?

4 I'm sorry. I'll repeat that. I'd like to know when she plans to visit our factory in Scotland.

a) I see. Is that all?
b) All right. I tell her. Is that the end?

5 No, not quite. I'd like to suggest a day, if she has no definite plans.

a) I see. Yes?
b) Yes? Suggest it.

6 The best time for us is the first Monday of next month. Have you got that?

a) Yes, of course I have. Now you will tell me your name and phone number again.
b) Yes, thank you. Could I have your name again and your phone number?

7 Jack Mellor. That's M–E– double L–O–R– And the number is two two four six three nine seven five seven. Oh… could she phone me today? Would you like me to repeat that?

a) No. That's all right. I've got all that.
b) No, don't repeat. I understand.

Now look at the message the receptionist took. Correct the mistakes and write it out again on the message pad.

TELEPHONE MESSAGE

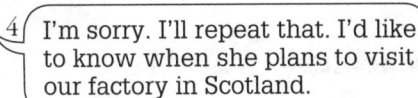
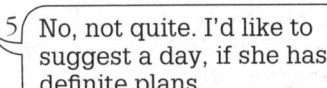

Miriam,
Jack Howatt from Mellor International called. He wants you to visit a factory in Scotland last week. He wants you to phone him today on (244) 369 575.

TELEPHONE MESSAGE

Grammar: questions/requests

2

Match the questions (1–5) with the answers (a–e).

1 (Could your grandmother speak German? _b_)

2 (Could you tell me where the board room is? ____)

3 (Could I speak to Tessa Saunders? ____)

4 (Could Einstein speak English when he was a child? ____)

5 (Could we meet on the 15th May? ____)

a) (Let me check my diary. Yes that's fine with me.)

b) (Yes, she could. She spoke five languages.)

c) (No, he couldn't. He learnt it in the United States in the 1930s.)

d) (Yes, of course. It's the second door on your left.)

e) (No, I'm afraid she's not in the office at the moment.)

3

Make questions.

1 you more slowly speak a little could
  <u>Could you speak a little more slowly?</u>   _R_

2 these letters into French could translate you before tomorrow
  _____
  _____ ____

3 English speak you could three years ago
  _____ ____

4 me you tell about the job something could
  _____
  _____ ____

5 these letters me for you could type
  _____ ____

6 you type five years ago could
  _____ ____

7 I Mr Knight could speak to please
  _____ ____

Now put R next to the questions that are really requests.

Vocabulary: travel

4

Complete the travel brochure with these words: _travel, trips, go on, get, journeys, cruises, flights_.

INTREPID TRAVELLERS LTD.

Do you (1) ___travel___ a lot on business or for pleasure? We have offers on business (2) _____ and longer (3) _____ by train or bus. We offer very competitive prices on (4) _____ to Africa, Asia and the United States with all the best airlines.

We also have special offers on (5) _____ to the Caribbean via the Canary Islands and Jamaica on the wonderful holiday ship, 'Queen Of The Oceans'.

If you want to (6) _____ a voyage of discovery or to (7) _____ a plane to your favourite holiday destination tomorrow, call us now on (071) 310 4987.

Vocabulary: *go on/take/ have/leave/ make*

5

Circle the correct words to complete these sentences. Sometimes two answers are possible.

1 I usually _____ a shower in the morning.
   a) go on b) have c) take

2 This morning I _____ a taxi to work.
   a) took b) went on c) had

3 Please _____ a seat. I'll be with you in a moment.
   a) have b) go on c) take

4 Last year my mother and father _____ a cruise to Hawaii and Bali.
   a) took b) went on c) had

5 Don't work so fast. _____ your time!
   a) Go on b) Have c) Take

6 It was a very good party. Everyone _____ a wonderful time.
   a) made b) took c) had

7 I'm afraid Ms Saunders isn't here. Can I _____ a message?
   a) have b) leave c) take

8 I see. She isn't there. Hmm. Could I _____ this message for her?
   a) give b) leave c) take

9 I don't want to fly to Paris. Let's _____ the train.
   a) have b) go on c) take

10 You work too much. Why don't you _____ a holiday?
   a) have b) take c) make

11 Last year I _____ a long journey to China.
   a) went on b) took c) made

Grammar: the future

6

Read the letter from Tom's sister and circle the correct alternative.

Dear Tom,

This is just a short letter because I **(1) am**/will be very busy at the moment. I **(2) will be/is** away next week on a business trip. I **(3) don't/won't be** back until 30th August. I **(4) am/will be** really happy that you are coming to Canada at Christmas. As you know, the weather **(5) be/will be** really cold at that time, so buy some really warm clothes. I usually **(6) will go/go** to the mountains to ski, but I **(7) will stay/stay** in Toronto to see you, of course.

Let me know your flight details and I **(8) will meet/meet** you at the airport. I am sure that Mother **(9) will be/is** happy to see you after so many years.

Love,

Hilary

Vocabulary: *-ing* and *-ed* adjectives

7

There are mistakes in seven of the sentences below. Cross out the mistake. Then write the correct word at the end of the sentence.

1 I am ~~interesting~~ in learning English. ____interested____

2 Could you explain that again? I'm very confusing. _____

3 I'm exciting about my new job. _____

4 Our boss is very worried about the sales figures. _____

5 I enjoy travelling, but it's very tired. _____

6 Bill can be very boring sometimes. He goes on and on talking but nobody wants to listen. _____

7 I don't want to watch this any more. I'm boring with it. _____

8 Do you think Stephen Spielberg's films are excited? _____

9 Bill isn't satisfying with his new car. _____

10 Do you want to hear my story? Are you interested? _____

Grammar: superlatives

1

Read this description. Then check the
summary below.

Word Master Computer Printer

Weight: 2.5 kilos (Similar printers weigh
more than 3 kilos)
Size: 400mm by 200mm (Other printers
500 mm by 300 mm)
Price: £300   (Similar printers cost
between £350 and £500)

Other Features

- Free Carrying Case (Case for similar
printers costs £50-60)
- Very quiet (Most other similar printers
are noisy)
- High quality of print (Quality of most
other printers not as good)

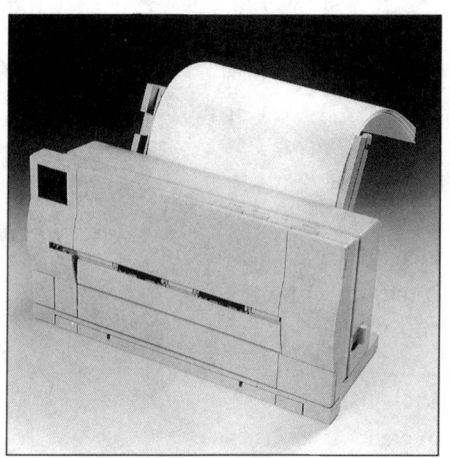

**There are five important mistakes here.
What are they? Cross them out.**

The new Word Master Printer is one of the ~~worst~~
and the heaviest printers on the market. It is also
one of the largest and most expensive. Its print
quality is one of the worst of all printers on the
market.

**Now correct the five mistakes. Write the
words that should be in the article.**

1   _best_
2   _____
3   _____
4   _____
5   _____

2

Complete these sentences. Use the
superlative form of these adjectives:
*big, expensive, common, high, rich,
popular, intelligent.*

1 The Queen is __the richest__ person in Britain.

2 China has _____ population in the
world.

3 Human beings are _____ mammals.

4 Finland is _____ country in the world.

5 'High Street' is _____ street name in
Britain.

6 Mount Everest is _____ mountain in
the world.

7 Smoked salmon is _____ food in
Harrods Food Halls.

Grammar: adjectives and adverbs

3

Complete the table.

Adjective	Adverb
immediate	1 immediately
2	fast
3	well
quick	4
successful	5
6	quietly
bad	7

Now circle the correct alternative.

1 We had a room at the back of the hotel so it was very *quiet/quietly* at night.
2 If Mr Knight rings, tell me *immediate/immediately*.
3 The company is very *successful/successfully* in Europe. They sell many of their products in twelve countries.
4 He is an excellent personal assistant. He types *quick/quickly* and speaks French very *good/well*.
5 I had a very *bad/badly* day at the office.

Vocabulary: *Go on, take* and *have*

4

Put ticks in the right columns.

	have	take	go on
1 a bath or shower	✓	✓	
2 a taxi			
3 a seat			
4 an aspirin			
5 a message			
6 an exam			
7 a coffee			
8 a flight			
9 a good time			
10 your time			
11 a journey			

In a meeting

5

Find the best response in the situations.

1 A: Now, this information is very important. Are you listening?
   B: a) Just a moment, please. I'd like to make some notes.
       b) Stop, please. I want to make notes.
       c) No, I'm not listening. I'm making some notes.

2 A: My pen isn't working.
   B: a) Here. I lend my pen.
       b) Here. You can lend my pen.
       c) Here. You can borrow my pen.

3 A: Would you like to use my pen?
   B: a) No, I don't want it.
       b) No, that's all right. Thanks all the same.
       c) I don't need it, but I give you the same thanks.

4 A: Oh, no! Look at my pen.
   B: a) What happens with it?
       b) What is happening to it?
       c) What's the matter with it?

5 A: This is one of the strongest, lightest bags you can buy.
   B: a) What's it made of?
       b) What's it like?
       c) What makes it?

6 A: Now, there's something more I think you should know about this. You see,…
   B: a) Yes? Go on, please. I'm listening.
       b) You will go on, please. I am listening.
       c) Do you go on? I listen.

Vocabulary: materials

6

Look at the names of these materials.

a) rubber
b) bricks
c) concrete
d) iron
e) glass
f) china

Now read these descriptions. Which material is it?

1 This material is transparent. In other words, you can see through it. Windows, bottles, cups and other containers are made of it. ___*e*___

2 We use them to build houses. They are rectangular and are often red or grey. _____

3 It is a hard grey material. It is used to make steel. _____

4 It comes from the juice of trees in hot countries. Tyres are made of it. Perhaps you have a small piece of it on the pencil you are using now. _____

5 This is a mixture of sand, stones and cement. It is a very hard strong material that is often used in tall buildings. _____

6 It is a hard white material and good quality cups and plates are made of it. _____

7

Study the dictionary definitions. Then look at the table of objects and materials below.

credit card /ˈkredɪt kɑːd/ *n* a card which allows you to obtain goods and services without using coins or notes; the cost is added to your account and you pay it later

jack·et /ˈdʒækɪt/ *n* a short coat

lad·der /ˈlædə/ *n* a wooden, metal, or rope frame with steps on it, which is used for climbing up and down things

rain·coat /ˈreɪnkəʊt/ *n* a light coat worn to protect yourself from rain

ser·vi·ette /ˌsɜːviˈet ‖ ˌsɜːr-/ *n BrE* a small square of cloth or paper which you use at meals to keep your clothes, fingers, and lips clean

so·fa /ˈsəʊfə/ *n* a comfortable seat long enough for two or three people to sit on

tights /taɪts/ *n* [pl] a very close-fitting garment made of thin material covering the legs and lower part of the body; tights are usually worn by women

watch /wɒtʃ/ *n* a small clock worn on your wrist: *My watch has stopped.*

Cross out the materials that don't belong.

Object	Can be made of:
watch	gold, plastic, leather, ~~cardboard~~
credit card	leather, plastic
tights	nylon, wood, cotton
sofa	suede, leather, paper
ladder	wood, nylon, aluminium, plastic
jacket	leather, suede, platinum, cotton
raincoat	plastic, nylon, suede
serviette	paper, cotton, leather

12

Conversation management

1

Read the conversations between A and B. What is the most polite thing B can say?

1 A: I'll finish the report next week.
   B: a) That isn't good enough. I want it sooner!
      b) Finish it sooner than that.
      c) Could you possibly do it sooner than that?

2 A: Can we meet next Wednesday?
   B: a) No, we can't. I'll be in Paris.
      b) I'm afraid I'll be in Paris then.
      c) No. I'll be in Paris. Suggest another day.

3 A: We could hold the meeting on Friday 14th at 10.30 at our head office.
   B: a) I don't understand.
      b) I'm sorry. Could you repeat that?
      c) I didn't understand. You have to speak more clearly.

4 A: You look pale. Are you feeling ill?
   B: a) No. What about you?
      b) No, I'm not. Why do you want to know?
      c) No, not at all.

5 A: Now, my next point is very important. You see, we have a problem with…
   B: a) Stop. I have a question.
      b) I'm sorry to interrupt but could I ask a question?
      c) Stop talking, please. I want to ask you a question.

6 A: Now, uh…you see…there's something I'd like to ask you but…uh…well…the problem is…uh…
   B: a) I see. Yes?
      b) What is it? Tell me.
      c) What are you talking about?

Grammar: *has/have to*

2

Read the advertisement below. Then complete the sentences below with these words: *have to, has to, can, will.*

Personal Assistant to Marketing Director

We are an international company with an excellent position for a young man or woman with a good knowledge of French and one of the two following languages: Spanish or Portuguese.

We *require someone to work closely with our Marketing Director. The hours are very long and it is necessary to travel and be away from home almost half the year. However, the salary is good and the work is extremely interesting.

For more information,
phone Denise (0734) 624 519.

*require: need; it is necessary to have
This job requires technical knowledge.

1 The Personal Assistant ___can___ be a man or a woman.

2 However, he or she _____ speak two languages.

3 One of these languages _____ be French.

4 However, the other language _____ be Spanish or Portuguese.

5 The Personal Assistant _____ work very long hours.

6 The Personal Assistant also _____ travel with the Marketing Director.

7 How many foreign languages _____ you speak?

8 Are you interested in this job? Phone Denise and she _____ give you more information about it.

9 But remember! In this job you _____ work very long hours. It's really necessary!

Grammar: *something/anything/ nothing*

3

Read the conversation. What are the missing words (1–8)?

A: I think there's (1) _something_ wrong with my car. Can you help me?

B: I'm sorry. I'd like to, but I don't know (2) _____ about cars.

C: I know (3) _____ about them. Perhaps I can help. What's the problem?

A: The engine won't start. When I turn it on, (4) _____ happens.

C: Hmm, perhaps (5) _____ is wrong with the electrical system. Let me see.

(Five minutes later)

A: Is it the electrical system?

C: No, that isn't the problem. (6) _____ is wrong with the electrical system at all.

A: Are you sure?

C: Yes, I am. It's (7) _____ different. And it isn't really a problem at all.

A: What do you mean?

C: It's the *petrol tank.

A: The petrol tank?

C: Yes, there isn't (8) _____ in it. It's empty.

* **petrol**: made from petroleum; what you put in the car
* **tank**: where you put the petrol

4

Make questions. Then match the questions (1–5) with the answers (a–e).

1 the what's matter
   What's the matter? _____ __d__

2 work why doesn't printer the
   _____
   _____

3 you would like to anything drink
   _____
   _____ _____

4 you what like would birthday for your
   _____
   _____ _____

5 breakfast what like would you for
   _____
   _____ _____

a) No, nothing thanks. I had a cup of coffee a few minutes ago.

b) There's something wrong with it.

c) Anything. A piece of toast or just a few biscuits will be fine, thanks.

d) Nothing at all. I'm just a bit tired.

e) Something very beautiful and very expensive!

Vocabulary: feelings

5

Use these words to describe the person's feelings in the pictures.

- depressed • disappointed • angry • afraid
- hopeful • worried • relaxed • pleased

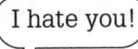

I hate you!

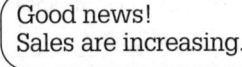

Good news! Sales are increasing.

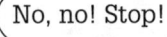

No, no! Stop!

Life is awful.

1 __angry__

2 _____

3 _____

4 _____

Perhaps I can get a good job, buy a car...

No money! What am I going to do?

I didn't get the job. I really wanted it, and I thought the interviewer liked me.

No problems, no stress today. I'm going to go for a walk and listen to some music.

5 _____

6 _____

7 _____

8 _____

Vocabulary: dimensions

6

Find the word that doesn't belong.

1	PEOPLE	tall	short	heavy	(high)
2	BRIDGES	tall	high	long	wide
3	ROADS	long	tall	wide	short
4	RIVERS	tall	wide	long	deep

Test 3

A Find the best alternative.

1 Mexico City is _____
   than Amsterdam.
   a) more big (b) bigger c) biggest

2 She lived in New York between 1983 and 1990,
   so she worked there _____.
   a) for seven years   b) seven years ago
   c) it makes seven years

3 I'm very _____ with my new computer.
   a) glad   b) happy   c) lucky

4 I hope you enjoyed your stay in our hotel,
   Mr Knight. _____
   a) Goodbye.   b) See you later.   c) Bye bye.

5 You look very tired. You _____
   to bed earlier.
   a) will go   b) have to go   c) should go

6 What did she _____ about the meeting?
   a) say   b) tell   c) talk

7 Kate doesn't know when the meeting is. Her
   boss didn't tell _____.
   a) she   b) her   c) him

8 _____ you answer the phone? I'm in the
   shower!
   a) Do   b) Should   c) Could

9 Last summer James went on a _____ to
   Greece.
   a) trip   b) travel   c) travelling

10 Take _____. I can wait.
   a) the time   b) your time   c) time

11 I'm sorry. _____
   a) What was your name again?
   b) Tell me your name.
   c) Please repeat your name.

12 _____ the traffic be very heavy at 6 pm?
   a) Don't   b) Isn't   c) Won't

13 She _____ in sport.
   a) is interesting b) has interest c) is interested

14 This cassette player _____. There's
   something wrong with it.
   a) doesn't function b) isn't well c) doesn't work

15 This chair is _____ chair in the office.
   a) the most comfortable
   b) most comfortable   c) more comfortable

16 Could you _____ me five pounds?
   a) borrow   b) lend   c) spend

17 He speaks Japanese very _____.
   a) good   b) well   c) better

18 These cups are made _____ plastic.
   a) in   b) from   c) of

19 I can't play tennis with you on Saturday. I
   _____ meet someone at the airport.
   a) have to   b) will   c) would

20 I don't want _____ to drink, thanks.
   a) anything   b) nothing   c) something

21 Please don't tell anyone about this. It's all very
   _____.
   a) public   b) important   c) confidential

22 What kind of _____ is this? Cotton,
   polyester or what?
   a) material   b) matter   c) clothes

23 She always says 'please' and 'thank you'. She's
   a very _____ person.
   a) educated   b) polite   c) rude

24 I worked all weekend to finish the report.
   Monday was the _____.
   a) finish   b) end   c) deadline

25 When I was younger I wanted to be a pilot.
   That was my real _____.
   a) ambition   b) job   c) work

Reading

1

Read the newspaper article. Then say which of the statements below are true (✔) and which are false (✘).

Hard Times Ahead for the Electronics Industry

In the 1970s and 1980s, profits in all branches of the electronics industry rose year after year. But things changed in the early 1990s and in the opinion of many experts they are going to get much worse before they get better.

'Products like the Walkman made extremely big profits five or ten years ago. There's nothing like that on the market today, but perhaps in a few years manufacturers can make very high profits again with mini-disc players or high-definition television,' Mr Mark Atwood-Wood, an analyst with Anglo-International Bank, said yesterday.

Computer manufacturers also have similar problems. Prices are falling by 20 per cent or more a year and competition is growing. Manufacturers, distributors and dealers have to accept lower profits each year. The result is that there is less and less money for investment in new products.

'Without investment in new products, the market cannot grow. But manufacturers can find enough money for investment only if the market grows by at least 15 per cent a year. That is not happening any more,' said Atwood-Wood.

1 Profits were better in the 1970s and 1980s than in the early 1990s. _✔_

2 Experts think that profits in the electronics industry will soon be very high again. ____

3 The article says that some companies are making very good profits from mini–disc players and high–definition television. ____

4 The article says that there is less and less competition for computer manufacturers. ____

5 *Consumer electronics* are things like television sets, video cameras and cassette players. ____

6 *Invest* means 'to put money in something with the hope that it will make a profit'. ____

7 Mr Atwood–Wood says that investment in new electronic products is very necessary. ____

8 He thinks that manufacturers will soon begin investing again in new products. ____

Vocabulary: things we can do with money

2

Complete the sentences with these words:
spend, lend, borrow, pay, cost, make, earn.

1 I think this new product will ___make___ a good profit.

2 Teachers don't _____ very good salaries in most countries.

3 Could I _____ some money from you?

4 Could you _____ me some money?

5 That's a very nice jacket. How much did it _____?

6 That's a very nice jacket. How much did you _____ for it?

7 How much money do you _____ on clothes every month?

Grammar: *will/going to*

3

Look at the pictures. Choose the best alternative to go with them: a or b.

1 ___Will you___ marry me?

   a) Will you   b) Are you going to

2 She _____ get married.

   a) will   b) is going to

3 Look! He _____ jump.

   a) will   b) is going to

4 _____ take this bag to the taxi,

please?

   a) Will you   b) Are you going to

4

Look at what A is saying (1–8). Find two good answers.

1 A: Will you marry me?
   B: a) Yes, I do.
      b) Yes, I will.
      c) I'm sorry but I don't love you.

2 A: The phone's ringing.
   B: a) I'll get it.
      b) Will you answer it, please?
      c) Yes, it is.

3 A: Do you think it's going to rain?
   B: a) Well, perhaps. Look at those clouds.
      b) I hope not.
      c) I don't hope.

4 A: Will you lend me some money?
   B: a) No, I don't lend it.
      b) It depends. How much do you want?
      c) I'd like to but I can't. Not this month.

5 A: Will you come to dinner with us this Friday?
   B: a) It's very nice of you to invite me.
         At what time?
      b) Yes, that's right.
      c) I'll be away then. Can we make it another
         time?

6 A: I'd like to speak to Kate Crawford, please.
   B: a) One moment. I'll put you through.
      b) Her line is engaged. Will you hold?
      c) Hold it! She's busy and can't talk to you.

7 A: When am I going to get your report, Roger?
   B: a) You wait. I finish.
      b) You'll have it before I leave this evening.
      c) I'll finish it as soon as possible.

8 A: Are you going to make some coffee?
   B: a) Yes, I am. Why? Would you like some?
      b) No, I won't. You will make it.
      c) No. Why? Did you want a cup?

5

Look at Tom's list of New Year's resolutions.

Resolutions for the New Year!
1 Give up smoking
2 Save money for new car
3 Buy some new clothes
4 Drink less
5 Eat less
6 Lose some weight
7 Live a more healthy life

Now write what Tom is going to do in the New Year.

1 Tom is going to give up smoking.

2 _____ money
   for _____.

3 _____ clothes.

4 _____ less.

5 _____ less.

6 _____ weight.

7 _____ a more healthy _____.

Vocabulary: *raise/rise/increase*

6

Study the definitions. Then look at the statements that follow.

> **raise** /reɪz/ *v* **raised raising** [T] **1** to lift or move something to a higher position: *Please raise your hands if you know the answer.* **2** to increase in amount, degree or size: *The company wants to raise the prices of some of its products and lower the price of others.*

> **rise** /raɪz/ *v* **rose risen** [I] **1** to go up or move to a higher position: *Prices rose last year by 3 per cent.* **2** to appear above the horizon: *In summer the sun rises around 4 am.*

> **increase** /ɪn'kriːs/ *v* **increased increasing 1** [I] to become larger in amount, number, or degree: *The population of this city increased by 50 per cent between 1984 and 1990.* – opposite **decrease**
> **2** [T] to make something larger in amount, number, or degree: *They are going to increase the price of petrol next month.* – opposite **reduce**

Which of these statements are true (✔) and which are false (✗)?

1 The symbol [**T**] means 'transitive' and the symbol [**I**] means intransitive. __✔__

2 Transitive verbs are verbs like *raise, lower, make, do.* We use transitive verbs to talk about a person or a thing doing something to another person or thing. _____

3 Intransitive verbs are verbs like *rise, fall, go, come.* We use intransitive verbs when a person or a thing does not do something to someone or something else. _____

4 Some verbs can be both transitive and intransitive. _____

5 The verb *increase* is only a transitive verb, never an intransitive verb. _____

6 The verb *reduce* is only a transitive verb, never an intransitive verb. _____

Now complete the sentences with these words: *increase, raise, rise.* Sometimes you can use two of the words in the same sentence.

1 Our prices are too low. We have to
   __increase/raise__ them.

2 When does the sun _____ in summer
   in your country?

3 How can we _____ our profits
   next year?

4 I think our profits are going to _____
   next year.

5 Did prices _____ very much last
   year?

6 If my boss doesn't _____ my
   salary, I'm going to leave!

7 Please _____ your head a little. Look
   at me!

8 Don't _____ your speed now.
   There's a police car behind you.

Grammar: Past/Present/Present Perfect

1

Someone is asking questions (1–9) at a job interview. Use these words (a–i) to complete the questions.

a) are you
b) have you been
c) were you
d) did you work
e) have you been working
f) do you work
g) have you been living
h) did you live
i) do you live

1 A: Where ___do you work___ now?

B: At Five Star Electronics. But I'm going to finish there at the end of the month. They're going out of business.

2 A: Yes, I heard something about that yesterday.

How long _____ there?

B: For about two years now.

3 A: And where _____ before that?

B: For Northern Computer Services in Manchester. They went out of business, too.

4 A: How long _____ there?

B: For seven years.

5 A: How long _____ in Manchester?

B: For twenty-eight years. I was born there.

6 A: Where _____ now?

B: Here in London. In Wimbledon.

7 A: How long _____ here?

B: For eighteen months.

8 A: Excuse me, but _____ married or single?

B: Married.

9 A: I see. And … I'm sorry to ask you these personal questions but _____ married very long?

B: No, not very long. For eighteen months now.

2

Name: Tom MacDonald
Profession: Engineer
Age: 29
Employer: Kenmay Electronics
Address: 18 Windham Avenue
London W 18

(29)	Age now
(27)	Left Toronto and came to live in London
(23)	Began working for Kenmay Electronics in Toronto
(22)	} MacGill University
(18)	
(14)	} High School in Toronto
(0)	Born in Toronto, Canada

Read the information about Tom. Then choose the correct words to complete these sentences below.

1 Tom _____ in London for two years.

a) lives   b) lived   (c) has been living

2 He _____ for Kenmay Electronics for six years.

a) works   b) worked   c) has been working

3 He _____ in Toronto for twenty-seven years.   a) lives   b) lived   c) has been living

4 He _____ at MacGill University for four years.

a) studies   b) studied   c) has been studying

5 He _____ to High School in Toronto for four years.

a) goes   b) went   c) has been going

6 He _____ born in Toronto twenty-nine years ago.

a) is   b) was   c) has been

3

Complete these sentences about Tessa Saunders.

Tessa Saunders is twenty-nine (1) __years__ old. She began (2) _____ for Knight and Day Advertising when she (3) _____ twenty-five. She has (4) _____ working there for four years now. She (5) _____ born in Liverpool, but for the last six years she has been (6) _____ in Wimbledon, a suburb of London. Before she (7) _____ her present job with Knight and Day, she (8) _____ for Bell and Winter, another advertising agency in London. She (9) _____ there for about eighteen months but was not very happy there.

Vocabulary: verbs and nouns

4

Complete this table

Verb	Noun
impress	1 impression
2	translation
connect	3
4	application
argue	5
6	investment
advertise	7
8	employment
interview	9

Now use words from the table to complete these sentences.

1 I have the ___impression___ that she doesn't like me.

2 Can you _____ these letters into English for me?

3 What's the _____ between work and money?

4 I would like to _____ for the job you advertised in yesterday's *Times*.

5 They never agree. They have lots of _____ .

6 Don't _____ your money in that company.

7 You can see lots of _____ in magazines.

8 My company _____ over five thousand people.

9 You can read the _____ with Tessa on page 56 of the Students' Book.

Vocabulary: words people confuse

5

Read these sentences. If they are correct, tick (✔) them. If they are wrong, write a cross (✗) next to them.

1 This is a very good hotel. I can advise it to you.
___✗___

2 I recommend you to buy a good dictionary. _____

3 All our prices enclose service. _____

4 We include our latest price list in this letter.
_____

5 The company's employers are on strike.
They want a wage increase. _____

6 You can take some bus to Victoria Station.
They all go there. _____

7 There isn't some water in the bottle.
Look. It's empty. _____

8 Anyone was looking for you. He didn't give
me his name. _____

9 I'm sorry, but I can't give you any information
about this. I don't know anything about it. _____

Now correct the mistakes in the sentences so that all of them are correct.

1 This is a very good hotel. I can recommend
it to you.

2 _____

3 _____

4 _____

5 _____

6 _____

7 _____

8 _____

Grammar: who/which

6

Fill in the gaps.

24 Belsize Gardens
London NW3
25 May

William Kettering
Personnel Manager
Yule and Campbell UK Ltd
Unity House
57 London Road
Reading RG6 1UH

Dear Mr Kettering,

I am writing to apply for one of the positions as salesperson (1) ___which___ you advertised in the Evening Standard on May 23.

I am a 21-year-old student. I will finish a Business Studies degree at Liverpool Polytechnic this June. Last summer I worked at Gambol and Smythe, a company in Liverpool (2) _____ manufactures bathroom fittings. Two years ago I worked with one of my older brothers (3) _____ has a job in the construction industry.

I am particularly interested in working for a company (4) _____ can provide me with sales experience.

I enclose two references: one from Mr Gambol, (5) _____ was my boss last summer, and another from Dr Ken Braithwaite, (6) _____ is Head of the Economics Department at my college.

I will be glad to send any other information you require.

I look forward to receiving your reply.

Yours sincerely,

Helen Wilcox

Helen Wilcox

Grammar: Present Perfect

1

Find the best response.

1 A: Have you ever been to Japan?

B:
a) No, I wasn't. Were you?
b) No, I don't want to be in Japan.
c) No, I haven't. Have you ?

2 A: Have you tried sashimi?

B:
a) I don't like to.
b) No, I haven't, but I'd like to.
c) Yes, I did. It was good.

3 A: Have you studied another foreign language?

B:
a) Yes. I studied French at school.
b) Yes. I have studied it.
c) Yes, I have to study another foreign language.

4 A: Have you met any American people?

B:
a) Yes. I have to meet them tomorrow.
b) No, I didn't meet them. Did you?
c) Yes, I met some last month. Why?

5 A: Have you read any good English books?

B:
a) No, I haven't. Could you recommend one?
b) No. I haven't read them. But I am going to.
c) Yes, I did. It was very interesting.

Grammar: verb forms

2

Look at this table. What are the missing forms?

Present	Past	–ing form	Past Participle
do/1 **does**	did	doing	done
eat/2	ate	eating	eaten
am/is/3	4 /were	being	been
5 /studies	studied	studying	studied
tell/6	7	telling	8
9 /10	read	11	12
13 /14	15	16	driven
see/17	18	19	20

3

One word in one of these sentences has the same pronunciation as the colour *red*. Circle the word with the same pronunciation.

1 Which newspaper do you read?

2 I usually read *The Times*.

3 Did you read *The Times* yesterday?

4 No, yesterday I read *The Daily Telegraph*.

4

All these pairs of words are in the past. Tick (✓) when the vowel sound is the same. Write a cross (✗) when the vowel sound is different.

1 sent read ✓
2 went sent ___
3 said read ___
4 read heard ___
5 heard were ___
6 meant read ___
7 meant learnt ___
8 learnt heard ___

5

Write the correct form of the verbs.

1 (*read*) What are you <u>reading</u>?

2 (*read*) Have you _____ this article?

3 (*do*) What kind of work do you _____?

4 (*do*) I've _____ all my work and now I'm going home.

5 (*be*) Where _____ you yesterday?

6 (*be*) Have you _____ to London before?

7 (*study*) Roger _____ science when he was at university.

8 (*study*) We have _____ your report very carefully.

9 (*tell*) Have you _____ anyone about this?

10 (*tell*) Yes, I _____ Tessa about it two days ago. Why?

11 (*drive*) Why are you _____ so fast? Slow down.

12 (*drive*) We've _____ a long way today. Let's stop.

13 (*see*) I _____ that film last year.

14 (*see*) I'm looking for Tessa. Have you _____ her?

Questions and answers

6

Make questions. Then match the questions (1–7) with the answers (a–g) below.

1 you a lie told ever have

    Have you ever told   a lie? __d__

2 this kind of exercise you before done have

    _____

   _____ before? _____

3 you long waiting been have

    _____

   _____ long? _____

4 to the interview a suit wear I should

    _____

   _____ interview? _____

5 financially well the company doing is

    _____

   _____ financially? _____

6 this company its employees pay well does

    _____

   _____ well? _____

7 you sashimi eaten ever have

    _____

   _____ ? _____

a) No, not really. I got here five minutes ago.
b) Yes. Sales are increasing and costs are down.
c) Yes. The salaries are very good.
d) No. Never. I've always told people the truth.
e) No, I haven't. What exactly is it?
f) Of course, I have. There are lots of them in this workbook.
g) Yes, I would advise you to. It always makes a good impression if you do.

Vocabulary: *say/tell, make/do*

7

Complete the sentences with the correct form of these words: *say, tell, make, do*.

1 I hope I __made__ a good impression on the woman who interviewed me.

2 I can't _____ the difference between these two things. Can you?

3 Tessa _____ 'Goodbye' and then left the office.

4 I think I've already heard that joke. Have you _____ it before?

5 Look at this letter. You've _____ a number of very serious mistakes.

6 Why are you _____ so much noise?

7 Have you ever _____ business with this company before?

8 I didn't know how to get here but a policewoman _____ me the way.

9 When I asked her, she _____, 'Turn right. Walk down the street and then turn left.'

Writing a formal letter

1

Choose the correct sentence (a or b) to use in a formal letter (for example, in a letter of application).

1 a) John Murray said I should write to you.
(b) I am writing to you on the recommendation of Mr John Murray.

2 a) As you know, Mr Murray is one of the directors of Murray and Greene.
b) You know him. He is one of the directors of Murray and Greene.

3 a) I worked for John a long time ago.
b) Mr Murray was my employer four years ago.

4 a) I liked working there a lot, but then I got a job in Canada, where I got a lot of good experience.
b) I was very happy there. However, I decided to take a position in Canada, where I gained very valuable experience.

5 a) I would like to inquire about the position you advertised.
b) Could you tell me something about the job?

6 a) I believe that my previous experience will be very useful in this position.
b) I've done a lot of this kind of work, so I think you should give me the job.

7 a) I enclose references from all my previous employers.
b) Here are the references from all the people I worked for before.

8 a) I will be available for an interview at any time.
b) I'll come in for an interview anytime you like.

9 a) I look forward to receiving your reply.
b) I am waiting for an answer to this letter.

Grammar: question tags

2

Make these sentences into questions.

1 You've done this before.
<u>You've done this before</u> , haven't you?

2 She's met Donald before.
She's _____ Donald before, _____ she?

3 We've met before.
We've _____ , _____ ?

4 You can meet him at the airport.
You _____ at the airport, _____ ?

5 He's studied English before.
He _____ English _____ ,
_____ ?

6 I met you at Jeff's party.
I _____ Jeff's _____ , _____ ?

7 You study English at the language school on the corner.
You _____
_____ , _____ ?

8 They've visited England before.
They _____ ,
_____ ?

Grammar: *has/is*

3

What does the *'s* represent. Is it *is* or *has*?

1 She's from Switzerland. ___is___

2 He's got a very good job. _____

3 She's finished the report. _____

4 It's raining. _____

5 It's been raining all day. _____

6 He's the Marketing Director. _____

7 Tom's booked his ticket. _____

8 Hilary's glad he's going to Canada. _____

Gap fill

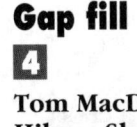

Tom MacDonald is phoning his sister, Hilary. She lives in Toronto. He lives in London. Complete their conversation.

TOM: Hi, Hilary. It's me. Tom.

HILARY: Hello, Tom. I (1) _haven't heard_ from you for ages!

TOM: What do you mean? I sent you a letter about five days (2) _____ . Didn't you (3) _____ it?

HILARY: No, it hasn't arrived (4) _____ . What (5) _____ your letter about?

TOM: Well, I wrote that I plan to (6) _____ to Toronto in December. I (7) _____ booked my ticket, but I (8) _____ collected it yet.

HILARY: That's wonderful, Tom. But how long (9) _____ you plan to stay here? I mean, (10) _____ you like to spend Christmas here with my family?

TOM: Well, your husband and children (11) _____ never met me before. How would they feel about having a stranger for Christmas dinner?

HILARY: Oh, they won't mind at all. I'm sure that all of them (12) _____ enjoy meeting you. When can you let me know what time you're (13) _____ arrive?

TOM: Perhaps tomorrow. I'll (14) _____ you as soon as the travel agent gives me all the necessary information.

HILARY: Wonderful! I'm really (15) _____ forward to seeing you again, Tom, after all these years.

Questions and answers

5

Match the questions (1–7) with the answers (a–g).

1 Have you had any experience of this kind of work? _f_

2 Does Tom speak French very well? _____

3 What's the matter with Dell Bradford? ___

4 Does Rosa enjoy her English classes? ___

5 Look at these figures. What do you think of the production costs? _____

6 Do you like Amsterdam? _____

7 Excuse me, but haven't we met somewhere before? _____

a) I don't know. But he seems to be angry about something.

b) Well, they don't seem to be going down.

c) Yes, it seems to be a very pleasant city.

d) No, I don't think so. At least, not that I can remember.

e) No. His pronunciation isn't very good and he makes lots of mistakes.

f) No, not exactly. But I have done things that were very similar.

g) Yes, she always seems to be very interested.

Find the mistakes

6

Tick (✔) the correct sentences. Put a cross (✘) next to the mistakes.

1 I met her for the first time for six years. **✘**

2 I've known her for six years. _____

3 I met them in April last year. _____

4 I knew Tom for the first time in April this year. _____

5 Kate knows Paris very well, doesn't she? _____

6 Kate speaks French good, isn't she? _____

7 Hilary's children and husband haven't met Tom yet. _____

8 I'd like to introduce you to my colleague, Kate Crawford. _____

9 How long do you know Kate? _____

10 How long have you known Tom? _____

11 The price of living is higher as it was last year. _____

12 The value of the American dollar is much lower than it was ten years ago. _____

13 Is this the first time you've done this? _____

14 This is the first time I drive this car. _____

Six of the sentences are incorrect. Can you correct them?

- _I met her for the first time six years ago._

- I _____

  _____

- Kate _____

  _____

- How _____

  _____

- The _____

  _____

- _____ the first time

  _____

Test 4

A Find the best alternative.

1 I had a really good weekend. I feel completely
_____ .
a) relax (b) relaxed c) relaxing

2 Roger can't go out tonight. He _____ a report.
a) has to finish b) has finished
c) have to finish

3 I'd love to go to the cinema with you. I haven't got _____ to do on Saturday night.
a) nothing b) something c) anything

4 How _____ is your brother?
a) tall b) high c) long

5 This box is really heavy. _____ help me?
a) Do you b) Will you c) Should you

6 He's not a very good typist. He _____ a lot of mistakes.
a) does b) commits c) makes

7 Mary is the woman _____ I met in Madrid last year.
a) that b) which c) what

8 I hope management decide to _____ our salaries.
a) rise b) raise c) arouse

9 How long _____ English?
a) do you study b) have you been studying
c) are you studying

10 It's a really simple machine. _____ can learn to use it.
a) No one b) Someone c) Anyone

11 Excuse me, I'm looking _____ Park Road. Can you tell me where it is?
a) for b) at c) to

12 To _____ the truth, I don't like sashimi very much.
a) say b) tell c) talk

13 Have you ever _____ a Ferrari?
a) drive b) drove c) driven

14 _____ the new Stephen Spielberg film yet?
a) Do you see b) Have you seen c) Are you seeing

15 She's Swedish, _____ .
a) isn't she? b) hasn't she? c) wasn't she?

B Fill in the gaps in the text.

BOOM YEAR FOR POIREL INTERNATIONAL

Profits rose more than forty per cent (1) _____at_____ Poirel International, the French educational software company, this year. Managing Director, Auguste Poirel, was delighted. 'The recession (2)_____ affected everybody, but we (3)_____ to be doing very well indeed!' he said when we (4)_____ him on Tuesday evening.

Poirel, 45, started the company fifteen years (5)_____ . Profits rose in the late seventies and early eighties, but began to (6)_____ in 1988. 'The company had a lot of problems with marketing and distribution. We appointed a new marketing director in 1989 and business (7)_____ been booming ever since.'

Poirel says that the company (8)_____ to increase production and expand its markets and to sell more software to the Asian and Australasian countries. 'Of course (9)_____ is a lot of competition from other software manufacturers with very good products on the market, but I think our software is better, cheaper and (10)_____ "user friendly". I'm sure we can compete!'